Daniel D. Pearlman | Anita DuBose

Letter Perfect
An ABC for Business Writers

Bobbs-Merrill Educational Publishing
Indianapolis
A publishing subsidiary of ITT

The Bobbs-Merrill Company, Inc.
4300 West 62nd Street
Indianapolis, Indiana 46268

First Edition
First Printing

Acquisition and development: Paul E. O'Connell
Copy editing and production: John Gastineau
Cover and interior design: Positive Identification, Inc.
Typesetting: Central Publishing Co.
Printing: Howard W. Sams Co., a publishing subsidiary of ITT

Library of Congress Cataloging in Publication Data

Pearlman, Daniel D.
  Letter Perfect

  1. English language — Business English — Handbooks,
manuals, etc. 2. English language — Rhetoric — Handbooks,
manuals, etc. 3. Commercial correspondence — Handbooks,
manuals, etc. 4. English language — Grammar — 1950–   — Handbooks,
manuals, etc. 5. English language — Usage —
Handbooks, manuals, etc. I. DuBose, Anita. II. Title.
PE1479.B87P42 1985   808'.066651   84-16756
ISBN: 0-672-61623-8

Table of Contents

The text is alphabetized according to the correction *symbol* (C, cap, case), not according to the full name of the writing problem.

Proofreading Symbols

These widely used symbols indicate errors in letter format, report format, or typing.

Symbol	Meaning
$\wedge$	insert copy shown
#	insert space
⌐	delete or omit
⌒	close up space
∿	transpose, turn around
¶	new paragraph
=/	insert hyphen
ss	single-space
ds	double-space
ts	triple-space
‖ or ≡	align copy
⟳	move copy as shown
. . . .	ignore correction
cap or ≡	capital letter
lc or /	lowercase letter
[⌐ ⌐]	move copy in the direction of bracket
⬭	spell out
___ or ital	underline or italicize
were / was	change as shown
⊙	make a period

insert a question mark

insert an exclamation point

insert a comma

insert a semicolon

insert a colon

insert an apostrophe

insert quotation marks

insert a dash

insert parentheses

indent 5 spaces

more space here

less space here

Preface

Business English texts have paid little attention to the process of revision that is so vitally important to the development of writing skills. *Letter Perfect* focuses on that process through a design that maximizes students' access to relevant information and minimizes the time they spend looking for it. We believe that the time students devote to the revision of a writing assignment should be spent mostly in actual *rewriting,* not in *research* through formidable reference books to track down the help they need. Yet business English texts are sorely lacking in "student-friendly" approaches that cut through the mounds of explanation and technicality that confront the student who is looking for the one simple rule applicable to an immediate sentence-structure problem.

Letter Perfect is a *short* guide and a true *ABC*; it is alphabetically organized to permit instant access to any specific point of information. The text also saves instructional time by encouraging the use of many common correction symbols in place of more elaborate marginal commentary. The practical emphasis of this text is carried out in the way each section is organized. First, students are referred by the correction symbols on their papers to the corresponding sections of the handbook. At the head of each section, a brief statement in large, colored print clarifies the symbol and tells students precisely what to *do.* An explanatory passage follows, but the focus is then on *how* to make the changes and less on the technical *why.* Wherever possible, a variety of complicated rules is reduced to a clear list or chart, such as those for the rules of usage governing capitalization or numbers. Particularly valuable are the examples that follow the briefly presented correction instructions. The examples are few, so as not to be overwhelming, and as representative as we could make them. To stress the concrete application of any abstract rule, the examples often include notes analyzing the specific problem they pose. Finally, to enable students to keep their own semester's record of their development as writers, we have included a number of diagnostically useful *Progress Charts* at the end of the manual.

Because the emphasis of *Letter Perfect* is on the problems of communication in today's business world, the student is often reminded of the need for cost-effective *brevity.* (This text aspires to be a model of exactly that.) Many sections stress also the need for *clarity, simplicity,* and good old-fashioned *correctness* in grammar and punctuation. In addition to such technical matters, the text gives considerable attention to *tone* or *attitude*, the need for tact and courtesy and for writing from the psychological perspective of the reader — not from the vantage point of the writer's own company or organization.

In spite of its small physical compass, *Letter Perfect* should serve as an effective alternative to the traditional voluminous business English textbooks because it contains an adequate treatment of all the essentials of business English style, usage, and mechanics. Even where a traditional textbook or reference work is assigned, this book, both concise and inexpensive, will provide the specialized instrument most students need for immediate help as they struggle to improve their business letters and reports.

Daniel D. Pearlman
University of Rhode Island

Anita DuBose

Letter Perfect

An ABC for Business Writers

When in doubt, do not abbreviate. Few abbreviations are acceptable in formal business writing.

Follow these rules:

1. **Titles.** Always abbreviate certain forms attached to personal names: Mr., Mrs., Ms., Dr., Jr., Sr., Esq., Ph.D., M.D.

2. **Organizations.** Use the commonly recognized initials of certain well-known organizations: FBI, ROTC, NBC, FFA, CIA. (No periods are needed.)

NOTE: When writers refer to themselves or their organizations with abbreviations, follow their lead. For example, if a writer signs herself Ms. J. L. Freeman or calls her company "the Jonson Corp.," use the same forms in answering correspondence.

3. **Business terms.** You may use certain well-known abbreviations on routine business forms such as packing slips, invoices, charts, and tables: ft., lb., oz., mph, mpg.

4. **Miscellaneous.** A number of miscellaneous expressions of two or more words are commonly abbreviated, usually by means of initial letters: i.e., e.g., A.D., p.m., wpm, R.S.V.P. (Small-letter abbreviations now tend to use no periods and no spaces: wpm, rpm, mph.) Consult a recent dictionary to be sure if a certain expression uses capital or lowercase letters and if it includes periods.

Be wary of these common abbreviation errors:

a. Avoid contractions, except in deliberately *informal* communications.

b. Avoid nonstandard short forms such as *thru* for *through, info* for *information,* or *X* for *exchange.* Do not use *&* for *and* unless it is part of an organization's name: Johnson & Sons.

c. Some abbreviations of single words may be easy to understand but are not yet acceptable in a formal business communication: dept. (department), cont. (continued), St. (Street).

adj | ADJECTIVE

Use an adjective or the correct form of an adjective.

An adjective modifies (describes) a noun or pronoun. Usually, an adjective occurs next to the word it modifies: the *delicious* coffee. But sometimes the adjective is separated from the word it modifies by one of a small class of verbs called *linking verbs*: The coffee smells delicious. The adjective *delicious* modifies the noun *coffee*. An adjective separated from the word it modifies by a linking verb is called a *predicate adjective*.

One common error in business writing is placing an adverb, instead of a predicate adjective, after a linking verb: The coffee smells *deliciously*. The most common linking verbs are all forms of *to be* (am, is, are, was, were, has been, have been, will be, would be, will have been, would have been), *to seem, to appear,* and the following verbs of the five senses: *to sound, smell, look, feel, taste.* Use an adjective, not an adverb, after a linking verb.

WRONG: Your report sounds *informatively.*
RIGHT: Your report sounds *informative.*

WRONG: Our burgers taste *scrumptiously.*
RIGHT: Our burgers taste *scrumptious.*

WRONG: He must feel *badly* to be out sick three days.
RIGHT: He must feel *bad* to be out sick three days.

CAUTION: Some linking verbs can also be used as normal *transitive* or *intransitive* verbs. Transitive verbs take a direct object. Intransitive verbs do not. The following examples should help prevent confusion:

LINKING VERB: The flower *smelled* fragrant. [*Fragrant* is "linked" to *flower.*]
TRANSITIVE VERB: I *smelled* the flower. [*Flower* is the direct object of *smelled.*]

LINKING VERB: She *felt* suspicious. [*Suspicious* describes the subject *she.*]
INTRANSITIVE VERB: She *felt* along the wall suspiciously. [Here the adverb *suspiciously* is correct. It is used to describe the physical action of feeling, not the mental state of the subject *she.*]

THE DIFFERENCE BETWEEN ADJECTIVES AND ADVERBS

It is usually easy to tell an adjective from an adverb. Most adverbs end in *–ly*. Adverbs may modify all verbs except linking verbs: He types *rapidly*. Adverbs may also modify adjectives (The guidelines are *intentionally* broad) and other adverbs (She works *unusually* hard). Some common adverbs do not end in *–ly: very, fast, slow, hard, well*. These same words, however, may also be used as adjectives, and only the context tells you what they are.

ADJECTIVE: The request came at the *very* end of the note. [*Very* is an adjective here because it modifies the noun *end.*]

ADVERB: The company was *very* successful. [*Very* is an adverb here because it modifies the adjective *successful.*]

ADJECTIVE: She is a *fast* typist. [Here *fast* is an adjective, modifying the noun *typist.*]

ADVERB: She types *fast*. [*Fast* is now an adverb because it modifies the non-linking verb *types.*]

ADJECTIVE: She looks *well*. [*Well* is an adjective here because it follows the linking verb *looks* and modifies the pronoun-subject *she.*]

ADVERB: She speaks *well*. [*Well* is an adverb here because it modifies the non-linking verb *speaks*. See also the following note on the difference between *good* and *well.*]

Feel (look) good versus feel (look) well: Use the adjective *well* when you mean a state of health. It is no compliment to tell your supervisor that she looks *well* today unless she has just recovered from an illness. If you simply mean that you admire her clothing, makeup, etc., tell her that she looks *good.*

CORRECT FORMS OF ADJECTIVES

1. Positive degree: The positive degree of an adjective is the simple form of the word: *great, proud, useful, lovely.* "The woods are *lovely, dark* and *deep,*" Robert Frost wrote.

2. Comparative degree: The comparative degree of an adjective is used when you compare two things. The comparative is usually formed by adding *–er* to adjectives of one syllable (great*er*, proud*er*) and by placing the word *more* before adjectives of more than one syllable (*more* useful, *more* salable).

EXCEPTION: Two-syllable adjectives ending in *–y* may also add *–er*: *lazier* or *more lazy, angrier* or *more angry, lovelier* or *more lovely.*

3. Superlative degree: The superlative degree of an adjective is used when you compare more than two things. Form the superlative by adding *–est* to the end of a one-syllable adjective (great*est*, proud*est*) and by placing the word *most* before adjectives of more than one syllable (*most* beautiful, *most* useful).

EXCEPTION: *laziest* or *most lazy,* etc. See comparative degree.

4. Irregular forms: The comparative and superlative forms of some adjectives are irregular. *Good* becomes *better* (comparative) and *best* (superlative); *bad* becomes *worse* and *worst*. The following correct examples illustrate the point:

* Henry is a good typist. [No comparison here]
* Henry is a better typist than Jim. [Comparison between two]
* Henry is the best typist in the office. [Comparison among more than two]

NOTE: Do not form the comparative or superlative twice:

WRONG: We will need a truck that is *more wider.*
RIGHT: We will need a truck that is *wider.*

adv | ADVERB

Use an adverb, or change the marked adverb to a more acceptable one.

An adverb modifies (describes) a verb, adjective, or another adverb. The form of an adverb is usually the adjective plus *–ly* (see ADJECTIVE for a discussion of exceptions).

WRONG: Sarah proofreads accurate.
RIGHT: Sarah proofreads accurately.

A few common problems with adverbs may easily be avoided:

1. Do not confuse *good* and *well*. *Well* is the adverb form of the adjective *good.* Use *well,* not *good,* to modify a verb.

WRONG: Three of the five applicants did *good* in their interviews.
RIGHT: Three of the five applicants did *well* in their interviews.

2. Do not misuse *sure* and *real*. These adjectives are often used informally as adverbs, but even adding *–ly* will not usually remove the awkwardness they create.

AWKWARD: I am *sure* glad you got in touch with me. [*Sure,* an adjective, is ungrammatically used to modify another adjective — *glad.*]
STILL AWKWARD: I am *surely* glad you got in touch with me. [*Surely* is now an adverb and can grammatically modify the adjective *glad,* but few people who speak or write native English will use such an unnatural combination as *surely glad.*]
IMPROVED: I am *very* glad you got in touch with me. [*Very* is an adverb, and *very glad* is an acceptable combination to the native speaker or writer of English.]

AWKWARD: The new typewriters function *real* well. [See explanation given for *sure.*]
STILL AWKWARD: The new typewriters function *really* well. [See explanation given for *surely.*]
IMPROVED: The new typewriters function *remarkably* (or *quite* or *exceptionally* or *unusually*) well.

3. Avoid double negatives.

A double negative is the use of two negative words in the same clause or sentence in such a way that they logically cancel each other out and make a *positive* statement instead: We are *not* going *no*where. The two negatives logically make a positive, and this sentence means, "We *are* going *some*where." The sentence should contain only one negative.

* We are *not* going *any*where.
* We are going *no*where.

In business writing, double negatives often occur with the adverbs *rarely, hardly,* and *scarcely.* These adverbs already have negative meanings by themselves.

WRONG: We can't hardly figure out these invoices.
RIGHT: We can hardly figure out these invoices.

WRONG: We haven't received scarcely one new catalog in three months.
RIGHT: We have received scarcely one new catalog in three months.

4. Do not use the adverbs *kindly* or *sooner* improperly.

AWKWARD: *Kindly* send us your next payment.
IMPROVED: *Please* send us your next payment.

AWKWARD: We would *sooner* ship your order ourselves.
IMPROVED: We would *rather* ship your order ourselves.

---

agr | AGREEMENT

1. Make the verb in your sentence agree in number with its subject.
2. Make the pronoun in your sentence agree with its antecedent.

1. SUBJECT-VERB AGREEMENT

If the subject is singular, make its verb singular: The *desk* [singular subject] between the wall and the cupboard *is* [singular verb] empty. If the subject is plural, make its verb plural: The *forms* [plural subject] you are mailing to the auditor *are* [plural verb] out of date.

In English, verbs have one form in all tenses except for the present tense. In the present tense, two endings are possible: with an *s* or without an *s*. If you choose the correct ending, your verb *agrees* with its subject. The following charts show you what endings to use with what pronouns and with the singular and plural of nouns:

PRONOUN-VERB AGREEMENT

I wake	He wakes
We wake	She wakes
You wake	It wakes
They wake	

NOUN-VERB AGREEMENT

SINGULAR SUBJECTS (NOUNS)	PLURAL SUBJECTS (NOUNS)
The machine works.	The machines work.
Susan works.	Susan and Fred work.
Democracy works.	Executives work.

Only the subject can govern the verb. Other words in the sentence cannot affect the verb. To find the subject easily, apply these hints:

a. The object of a preposition cannot be the subject: This *report* on automobile accidents *is* not up to date. [*Report* is the subject, not *accidents*. *Accidents* is the object of the preposition *on* in the prepositional phrase *on automobile accidents*. *Report* takes the singular verb *is.*]

RECOGNIZING PREPOSITIONS: A preposition is a word or short sequence of words that is always linked to some form of noun or to a pronoun in the objective case. The noun or pronoun linked to the preposition is called the *object* of the preposition. The object usually follows the preposition.

EXAMPLES: for the moment [*For* is the preposition; *moment* is the object.] because of him [*Because of* is the preposition; *him* is the object.]

A preposition relates its object to another word in the sentence.

* We left the ledger *on top of* the file cabinet. [The preposition *on top of* relates its object *file cabinet* to the verb *left,* indicating *where* something was left.]
* Buying stock is an act *of* faith. [The preposition *of* relates its object *faith* to the noun *act,* giving specific character to the abstract noun *act.*]

A *prepositional phrase* includes a preposition, its object, and all of the words that modify (describe) the object.

EXAMPLE: because of a long and distinguished career [The words *a long and distinguished* modify the object *career.*]

A LIST OF COMMON PREPOSITIONS

about	due to	over
above	during	regarding
according to	except	through
after	for	to
against	from	toward
at	in	under
because of	in case of	until
before	instead of	up
behind	like	with
below	of, off	with regard to
by	on	within
concerning	out	without

b. *There, here,* and *where* are not subjects. When these words come before the verb, the subject *follows* the verb: Where *are* the Colson *files?* [*Files* is the subject and takes the plural verb *are.*]

c. Subjects connected by *and* are plural: A *typewriter* and an *adding machine* were missing. [Two things linked by *and* are the subject here.]

EXCEPTIONS: With the indefinite pronouns *each* and *every,* even subjects that are logically plural become grammatically singular, and the verb must agree with the singular *each* and *every*: *Each* typewriter and adding machine *was* accounted for.

When the items connected by *and* form only one logical subject, the verb also must be singular: Macaroni and cheese *is* my favorite food. [Macaroni and cheese *is* one dish.]

When subjects are connected by *or, nor, either . . . or, neither . . . nor, not only . . . but also,* make the verb agree with the nearest subject.

- Neither price nor selling *features were* a factor.

- Neither selling features nor *price was* a factor.

2. PRONOUN-ANTECEDENT AGREEMENT

The antecedent is the word that a pronoun stands for. A singular antecedent takes a singular pronoun. A plural antecedent takes a plural pronoun.

- My *word processor* seems to have lost *its* memory. [*Word processor* is singular and takes the singular pronoun *its.*]

- Our *managers* have just finished *their* computer reports. [*Managers* is plural and takes the plural pronoun *their.*]

NOTE: A company or organization is singular and takes the singular pronoun *its*: Aerodynamic Subsidiaries has *its* own engineering department.

Indefinite pronouns and the problem of sexism. A special problem in the use of pronouns may occur when the following words, called *indefinite pronouns,* are used as antecedents: *each, every, everyone, everybody, everything, someone, somebody, anybody, no one, nobody, either, neither, another.* Although they may occur in a sentence as antecedents, these words are themselves singular pronouns and should be referred to by singular pronouns. Note also that they take singular verbs.

- *Each* of us knows *his* job. [The use of *his* assumes that *us* consists entirely of males.]
- *Each* of the women presented *her* opinion.

NOTE: When any of these antecedents stands for a group of both men and women, you have several options:

a. You may use a double pronoun: Each of us knows *his or her* job very well. Since double references can get cumbersome if overused, try these alternate ways to represent both male and female in a group:

b. Leave out the pronouns entirely where possible.

CORRECT: Everyone made *his or her* presentation.
BETTER: Everyone made a presentation.

c. Use plurals where possible.

CORRECT: Everyone made *his or her* presentation.
BETTER: *All managers* made *their* presentations.

See also SEXIST EXPRESSION.

---

apos I APOSTROPHE

Add a missing apostrophe ('), or remove one you have mistakenly used.

The apostrophe has three uses:

1. to show contraction
2. to show ownership
3. to show the plural of letters, abbreviations, and numbers

1. CONTRACTIONS

Although you should avoid contractions (*I'm, can't, don't*) in formal business writing, you will occasionally want to use them in *informal* settings. Use an apostrophe to stand for the parts of words missing in a contraction: *I'd* (I would or I had), *we've* (we have), *aren't* (are not). A common error is to place the apostrophe where two words are joined: *Could'nt* is wrong, whereas *couldn't* is right.

Its and It's. *Its* is a possessive pronoun and *it's* is a contraction of two words (*it is* or *it has*). Use *it's* when you can make that word into two words.

WRONG: *Its* time for a change.
RIGHT: *It's* time for a change. [*It's* means *it is.*]

WRONG: The company honored *it's* vice-president.
RIGHT: The company honored *its* vice-president. [*Its* means "belonging to *it*" or "the company."]

2. OWNERSHIP

Should you write *attorneys* or *attorney's*? If you mean more than one attorney, a simple plural, write *attorneys*: The company has fifteen full-time attorneys. But if the idea of ownership is involved, write *attorney's*, which is the possessive case and means *belonging* to or *of* an attorney: The attorney's office was neater than her car.

A simple test for the possessive case: Put the word that is giving you trouble into an "of" phrase. Should you write *dogs bone* or *dog's bone?* If an "of" phrase, *bone of the dog,* sounds logical, then use the apostrophe: *dog's bone.* If you are talking about *more than one dog,* however, use the following two suggestions to distinguish between the possessive singular and the possessive plural:

a. Possessive singular: Add –'s. "The *dog's* bone" means "the bone of the dog" (one dog).

b. Possessive plural: add –s'. "The *dogs'* bones" means "the bones of the dogs" (several dogs). (A number of plurals do not end in –s. In the possessive, treat them like the singular: *children's.*)

PLURALS OF LETTERS, ABBREVIATIONS, AND NUMBERS

Use the apostrophe for the following:

a. Plurals of *lowercase* (small) letters: *p's* and *q's.* Plurals of *capital* letters allow you a choice: *Qs* or *Q's.* (But use *A's, I's,* and *U's* to avoid confusion with the words *As, Is,* and *Us.*)

b. Plurals of abbreviations that include periods: *M.B.A.'s, Ph.D.'s.* Abbreviations with no periods allow you either of *two* options: *VIPs* or *VIP's.*

c. Plurals of numbers: here, again, you have two options: *20's* or *20s, 1980's* or *1980s.* Once you choose a style, stick to it throughout that piece of writing.

Rethink and rewrite the passage in question.

Awkward is a catchall term used when a sentence or a series of sentences goes wrong. It may refer to a single problem such as a faulty phrase or to a general lack of coherence over an entire paragraph.

Sometimes *awkward* points to a more specific problem, such as choppy sentences, repetition, or faulty parallelism. By using the term *awkward,* your instructor probably feels that the error will be apparent to you at a glance and does not need a more technical name. If you do not see any problem with the marked passage, make an appointment to see your instructor as soon as possible to discuss it. If you do see something wrong, use your own judgment to rewrite it.

A passage may contain so many different problems that your instructor will mark it *awkward* rather than list each separate problem. In rewriting, avoid working with the same troublesome passage. Instead, start over again. Think back to the idea you were originally trying to express and form your sentences anew. Rethink ideas as well as rewrite them.

The following sentences may shed some light on a passage marked *awkward* in your own writing:

AWKWARD: The first step in producing is materials.
REVISED: The first step in producing is acquiring the right materials. [The problem was the lack of a complete idea.]

AWKWARD: With every attempt the manager made to explain the delay made the customer more angry.
REVISED: Every attempt the manager made to explain the delay made the customer more angry. [The problem here was a *mixed construction.* The writer simply forgot that the sentence began with *with.* See MX.]

AWKWARD: Seeing that the expenditure for copper has increased enormously during the past ten years and that inflation has continued to rise provides a new price increase.
REVISED: Since the expenditure for copper has increased enormously during the past ten years, and since inflation has continued to rise, we must increase our prices. [The sentence is relatively long and the writer simply lost control over the grammatical *structure.* Once the writer rethinks the idea, the obvious structure of two subordinate clauses — *Since* . . . and *since* . . . — followed by a main clause — *we must* . . . — emerges out of the original word heap.]

Add brackets here, or change these incorrect brackets to parentheses.

1. Use brackets to insert remarks or editorial corrections in quoted material: The production manager said, "May 3 [he had originally told us June 3] is the deadline for the report."

2. Use brackets around the italicized term *sic* (meaning *thus*) to show that an error in quoted material was *thus* in the original document. Since quotation must be exact, this is the only way to indicate that the error was not made by the quoter: The memo stated: "The principle [*sic*] reason for the decline in sales is uneven distribution." *Sic* points out the misspelling of *principal*.

3. Use brackets to avoid putting parentheses within parentheses: Ross Webber's book is required reading for this course (*Management: Basic Elements of Managing Organizations* [Homewood, Illinois: Richard D. Irwin, 1979]).

4. Do *not* use brackets in place of parentheses.

WRONG: Insert proofreaders' marks [see specimen pages 4, 5] in the margin opposite the error.

NOTE: Do not use brackets to insert remarks in material you are *not* quoting. See rule 1.

RIGHT: Insert proofreaders' marks (see specimen pages 4, 5) in the margin opposite the error.

C I COMMA

Only six rules cover almost every use of the comma:
1. Use a comma to prevent misreading.
2. Insert a comma before a coordinating conjunction that connects two main clauses.
3. Insert a comma after sentence elements that appear before the main clause.

4. Insert commas between words, phrases, and clauses in a series.
5. Insert commas between coordinate adjectives.
6. Use commas to set off parenthetical (*nonrestrictive*) sentence parts.

1. COMMA TO PREVENT MISREADING

- If tired, typists often make mistakes.
- Several days after, I understood that she was gone. *Or:*
- Several days after I understood that, she was gone.

2. COMMA BEFORE A COORDINATING CONJUNCTION THAT CONNECTS TWO MAIN CLAUSES

A main clause contains a subject and a verb and can stand alone as a sentence.

MAIN CLAUSE: The terms of the lease are very generous. [Subject: *terms.* Verb: *are.*]
MAIN CLAUSE: The service contract charges are unusually high. [Subject: *charges.* Verb: *are.*]

Coordinating conjunctions (*and, but, or, nor, for, yet*) are often used to connect two main clauses, but a comma should be placed before the conjunction.

- The terms of the lease are very generous, *but* the service contract charges are unusually high.
- We do not consider the current inventory dangerously low, *nor* do we reorder until the weekly count on Monday.

EXCEPTION: When a main clause is very short, you may omit the comma: He did the sorting and she did the collating.

3. COMMA AFTER SENTENCE ELEMENTS BEFORE THE MAIN CLAUSE

Use a comma after everything that comes *before* the main clause — except short prepositional phrases and brief adverbs of time.

- Before I make any appointments, I check my calendar. [Comma after subordinate clause.]
- Persisting, we succeeded. [Comma after a verbal, a word that comes from a verb.]
- In the midst of a general market slump, Wolf Industries showed unusually high profits. [Comma after *long* prepositional phrase. BUT note the following: *In June Wolf*

Industries showed a profit. No comma is needed after the short prepositional phrase *in June.*]

* In fact, Wolf gains surprised even its own top management. [Comma after a transition. Although *in fact* is a short prepositional phrase, it is one of a group of expressions called *transitions*. A transition is a logical bridge between ideas. Transitions are always set off from the rest of the sentence by commas, whether they occur at the beginning, middle, or end of the sentence. See TRANSITIONS]

* Yesterday the computer broke down. [No comma needed after a brief adverb of time such as *yesterday, last week, a month ago.*]

4. COMMAS BETWEEN WORDS, PHRASES, AND CLAUSES IN A SERIES

The use of commas within a series of items can be represented as follows: This company's priorities are people, product, and profit.

In business punctuation, the comma before the conjunction *and* is always used.

* The bid was overpriced, underdesigned, and inaccurate. [A series of adjectives.]

* In the morning I open all the mail, sort the messages, take a coffee break, then type the daily route assignments. [A series of verb phrases, or *predicates*. The conjunction *and* is implied, not stated: *and then type,* etc.]

* Either Joan, Chris, or Michael will make the changes you request. [A series of nouns.]

* My latest survey shows that we are low on typing paper, that we are overstocked on correction fluid, and that we are just about out of manila envelopes. [A series of subordinate clauses beginning with *that.*]

* We are in the black, our competition fears us, and our morale is very high. [Three main clauses.]

NOTE: When *all* items in a series are connected by coordinating conjunctions, do *not* use commas: They gave their time *and* effort *and* love.

5. COMMA BETWEEN COORDINATE ADJECTIVES

Use a comma to separate coordinate adjectives — a series of adjectives that stand in *equal* relation to the noun they modify. To find out whether adjectives are coordinate (and should be separated by a comma), write *and* between them. If the result sounds acceptable, the adjectives are coordinate.

* Who developed this *clever, amusing* sales campaign? [Acceptable: "clever *and* amusing sales campaign." Use a comma.]

Sometimes adjectives stand in *unequal* relation to the noun they modify and are not separated by a comma.

* This is an *amusing advertising* gimmick. [Unacceptable: "an amusing *and* advertising gimmick." Do not use a comma.]

6. COMMAS TO SET OFF PARENTHETICAL (NONRESTRICTIVE) SENTENCE PARTS

Set off parenthetical — also called *nonrestrictive* — sentence parts with commas. Information not essential to the meaning of a sentence is parenthetical. In the following sentences, parenthetical elements appear in italics. If you read these sentences without the italicized words, the essential meaning of each remains intact. Thus, the italicized words are parenthetical, and parenthetical elements must be set off with commas.

- Our personnel director, *Mr. Grinnell,* will be back Tuesday. [The essential meaning is preserved if you read, "Our personnel director . . . will be back Tuesday."]

- The opportunity for self-realization, *even more than the lure of financial reward,* is the single most important factor contributing to job-satisfaction.

- The publication date, *which was originally set for June,* has been postponed to December.

Restrictive sentence elements: Information essential to the meaning of a sentence is *restrictive.* In the following example, the italicized words cannot be dropped without distorting the essential meaning. Thus, they are *restrictive* elements and are *not* set off with commas.

- All employees *who have perfect attendance for the quarter* will receive a $100 bonus. [Try reading the sentence without the italicized words: "All employees . . . will receive a $100 bonus." Since the essential meaning of the sentence is now distorted, the italicized portion is restrictive and is *not* set off with commas.]

Specialized uses of commas for the inclusion of additional information in a sentence:

a. Commas to set off a state (or country) after a city:

- Toledo, Ohio, is called the Glass Capital of the World.
- This silver set was made in Taxco, Mexico.

b. Commas to set off the parts of a date:

- On Tuesday, May 16, 1983, our committee submitted its findings.

c. Commas to set off *Inc./Incorporated* and *Ltd./Limited* in company names:

- Havilchek, Inc., is the name of our newest overseas branch.

d. Status terms and titles after a person's name:

- Martin Paine, Jr., & Company does all our graphics.
- Sarah Wilcox, Ph.D., has agreed to present the keynote address.
- Kurt Frishmann, vice-president of marketing, will chair the committee.

e. Dialogue and question "tags":

- "Not many of you," she said, "have seen the latest bill of materials." [See also QUOTATION MARKS.]
- Carole took her portfolio with her, didn't she?

f. Commas to set off *direct address* — calling someone or something by name:

- Taxpayers, unite against government bureaucracy!
- Please get the invoice batch for today, Jim, because we just received some additions.

cap | CAPITALIZATION

Capitalize the word(s) shown, or substitute a lowercase letter if you have used capitals by mistake.

1. THE GENERAL RULE

Capitalize all proper names. Proper names identify specific persons, places, things, times, races, organizations: *Bill Farmer,* the *Amazon River, Coca-Cola, Brooklyn College,* the *Organization of American States,* the *Second World War.* Do not capitalize the word *the* introducing names of events or organizations: *the* Crimean War, *the* United Nations.

EXCEPTION: If the organization itself capitalizes *The* in its title, follow the usage of that organization.

2. SPECIFIC RULES

There are so many specific rules for capitalization that we have broken them down into an alphabetized list.

1. Acts, laws, treaties: the Constitution of the United States, the Bill of Rights.
2. Astronomical bodies: Venus, Jupiter, Mars. Also Earth, Sun, Moon *only* when named as specific astronomical bodies.
3. Brand names: Coca-Cola, Teflon. Do not capitalize the common name of the item that follows the brand name: Adidas sneakers, *not* Adidas Sneakers.
4. Complimentary close, first word of: Very truly yours.
5. Course titles: I'm taking Economic Theory II. Do not capitalize references to the field of study as such, unless it includes words that are normally capitalized: I'm majoring in economics. I'm interested in American history.
6. Days of the week: Monday, Friday.

7. Departments or divisions of one's own organization beginning with *the*: This is for the Accounting Department. *But*: This is from our accounting department, and this is from the accounting department at your former company.

8. Direct address: Tell me, Friends, what can I do for you?

9. Family titles without modifiers: Mom, Mother. *But* my mom, your mother.

10. First word of every sentence and every quoted sentence: He said, "Pay me half now, half later."

11. Government bodies: the Boston City Council, the United States Supreme Court, the Board of Education (if a specific city or state board is meant).

12. Historical events and periods: World War II, the Middle Ages.

13. Holidays: New Year's Eve, the Fourth of July, Mother's Day.

14. Hyphenated words: mid-Pacific, non-European. Capitalize the words you would capitalize in any other context.

15. Languages: English, Spanish, Arabic.

16. Months of the year: July, April.

17. Nicknames: the Rockies, the City of Brotherly Love, the Big Apple.

18. Noun + number combinations: Flight 124, No. 870, Figure 10. *But*: page 8, line 3, note 5, paragraph 7, verse 23.

19. Organizations: Our Lady of Hope Church, the Jonson Brothers Company. Capitalize *the* only when you write the organization's address.

20. Personal names: Sue, Anne DeLucca. But follow the individual's preference: Anne *de* Lucca.

21. The personal pronoun *I*: I think; therefore I am.

22. Places: Fifth Avenue, Salt Lake City, the Ohio River, USSR, Hotel Hide-a-Way.

23. The President and cabinet members: Today the President appointed his new Secretary of Defense. (For titles of other officials, see item 30.)

24. Proper adjectives: American, Hawaiian. In certain phrases, however, proper adjectives have lost their original meaning and are not capitalized: venetian blinds, panama hat.

25. Races, peoples: the Chinese, Hispanics, the Blacks. *But*: the black race.

26. Regions of the country and their inhabitants: the South, the West Coast, a Southerner. But do not capitalize compass directions: Go three blocks west.

27. Religions (and adjectives formed from them): Islam (Muslim), Judaism (Judaic, Jewish), Protestantism (Protestant), Catholicism (Catholic).

28. Salutations: Dear Mary, My dear Friend, . . . (Capitalize the first word and all nouns.)

29. References to the Supreme Being and sacred books: God, the Messiah, Our Lord, the Bible, the Koran.

30. Titles of officials when preceding a name: Mayor Dubuque, Vice-President Smith. *But*: I wrote to the mayor; I spoke to your senator.

31. Titles of books, journals, articles, movies, plays, headings in reports: Capitalize the first and last word and every word except unimportant connectives (*and, the, from,* etc.) shorter than five letters: *Life with Father, A History of Greece, The Old Man and the Sea.*

case | CASE

Use the correct case of the pronoun.

Many of the errors you make in *case* are carryovers of informal speech patterns into the more formal situation of writing, where a high degree of grammatical accuracy is usually expected.

Case is the form a pronoun takes when performing a certain role in a sentence. Three cases exist in English: the subjective case, the objective case, and the possessive case. (For *nouns* in the possessive case, see APOSTROPHE.)

Here are the cases of pronouns in chart form:

PRONOUN CASES

SUBJECTIVE	OBJECTIVE	POSSESSIVE
I	Me	My, mine
We	Us	Our, ours
You	You	Your, yours
He	Him	His
She	Her	Her, hers
It	It	Its
They	Them	Their, theirs
Who, whoever	Whom, whomever	Whose

The following examples show how pronouns change their form if they change their grammatical role (case) in sentences:

We hired *her* last week.
Subj.   Obj.

She hired *us* last week.
Subj.   Obj.

How do you know what case of a particular pronoun to use? That depends mainly on your ability to recognize the positions of subjects and objects in sentences. You probably have fewest problems with the possessive case, and those are usually spelling problems.

Using the subjective and objective cases: In a simple sentence such as "She hired him," we see the typical English sentence pattern: subject (*She*) + verb (*hired*) + direct object (*him*). To use case correctly, use the subjective case in positions occupied by subjects and the objective case in positions occupied by objects. Two other sentence positions occupied by *objects* are important to note: *indirect objects* and *objects of prepositions*.

Verbs may have not only direct objects but also indirect objects: She gave *him* (*her, me, us,*) a job. You can tell when *him* is an indirect object if you can "translate" it to mean *to him* or *for him*: She gave *him* a job = She gave a job *to him*.

Another position for objects is after prepositions (*to, for, of, by, with,* etc. Prepositions are discussed under AGREEMENT.). When the object of a preposition is a pronoun, it must be in the objective case.

* They voted for *him* and *me*.
* To *whom* are you writing this memo?

COMMON CASE PROBLEMS

1. The double subject. Do not use the objective case in double subjects.

ERROR: Him and Claire signed the receipt.
REVISED: He and Claire signed the receipt. [The subjective case *he* is correct. To test for the correct case, drop "and Claire." "Him . . . signed" sounds wrong.]

2. The double object. Do not use the subjective case in double objects.

ERROR: Kate telephoned both Suzanne and *he*.
REVISED: Kate telephoned both Suzanne and *him*. [*Him* is a direct object. To test for the correct case, drop "both Suzanne and." "Telephoned . . . he" sounds wrong.]

ERROR: Bill gave her and *I* the information.
REVISED: Bill gave her and *me* the information. [*Me* is an indirect object.]

ERROR: They returned the audit to Myra and *I*.
REVISED: They returned the audit to Myra and *me*. [*Me* is object of a preposition.]

3. Pronoun + appositive as subject. Use the subjective case for sentences beginning with a pronoun plus an appositive in the subject position.

ERROR: *Us* typists are very practical people.
REVISED: *We* typists are very practical people. [*Typists,* part of the subject of this sentence, is an *appositive,* a noun that renames or identifies the noun or pronoun before it. If you drop the appositive *typists,* you can see that "Us . . . are very practical" sounds wrong.]

4. Than/as + pronoun. Use the subjective case for comparisons ending with a pronoun intended as a subject.

ERROR: Hilary spells better than *me*.

REVISED: Hilary spells better than *I*. [The sentence would logically continue as "Hilary spells better than *I do*" or "than *I spell*." The subjective case — *I* — is needed because the pronoun after *than* is the subject of an elliptical (unfinished) clause *I spell*.]

ERROR: Joan is as intelligent as *him*.

REVISED: Joan is as intelligent as *he*. [Think: "as *he is*." *He* is the subject of the elliptical clause *he is*.]

NOTE: If the pronoun after *than* or *as* is intended as the *object* of the omitted verb, then it should be in the objective case:

- John likes him better than *me*. [Think of the sentence with the full elliptical clause included: John likes him better than *he likes me*.]

5. "To be" + subjective case.
Use the subjective case for any pronoun immediately following the verb *to be* (*am, is, are, was,* etc.).

ERROR: It was *her* who borrowed my new calculator.

REVISED: It was *she* who borrowed my new calculator.

6. Who (whoever)/ whom (whomever).
In choosing between *who* (*whoever*) and *whom* (*whomever*), use *who* if the pronoun you want is the *subject* of its own clause. Use *whom* if the pronoun you want is an *object* in its own clause:

- *Who* gave me the flowers? [Correct. *Who* is the grammatical subject of this question.]
- *Whom* are you angry with? [Correct. If you turn the sentence around, you get "You are angry with *whom*?" and you can see that *whom* is object of the preposition *with*.]
- She avoided *whoever* upset her. [Correct. You would expect the object of the verb *avoided* to be *whomever*. It is not. The object of *avoided* is the whole clause *whoever upset her*. *Whoever* is correct because it acts as the *subject* of its own clause, *whoever upset her*.]

7. Whose/who's and its/it's.
Do not confuse certain forms of the possessive case with contractions. *Whose* and *its* imply *possession* or *ownership*.

- *Whose* price list is this?
- Take the camera out of *its* case.

Who's and *it's* are contractions and are used informally to replace *who is* and *it is*.

- *Who's* [*Who is*] the culprit responsible for this vandalism?
- *It's* [*It is*] your last chance.

For *nouns* in the possessive case, see APOSTROPHE.

8. Possessive case before gerund. Use the possessive case before a gerund (a word ending in *–ing* that acts as a noun). Look at the following sentence:

* *Buying* and *selling* take up most of my working day.

The words *buying* and *selling* are gerunds because they act as nouns (subjects of the sentence). The word *working,* although an *–ing* word, acts as an adjective modifying *day* and is therefore not a gerund. A common error is the use of the objective case before a gerund.

ERROR: Mr. Byrnes forgot about *him* arriving today.
REVISED: Mr. Byrnes forgot about *his* arriving today.

ERROR: I look forward to *us* collaborating on the project.
REVISED: I look forward to *our* collaborating on the project.

---

choppy | CHOPPY SENTENCES

Revise short, choppy sentences by varying your sentence patterns.

Sentences sound "choppy" when several in a row are monotonously similar in *length* (all short, usually) and repetitive in *structure* (usually a series of simple sentences of the subject-verb pattern or the subject-verb-object pattern). Their rhythm lacks variety.

Revising a series of choppy sentences means more than connecting them with *ands* and semicolons. Such cosmetics will not hide a monotony of structure and rhythm that would simply be apparent in longer sentences. If, however, you *vary* the structure of your sentences and use effective *transitions,* you will rapidly develop a smoother style.

CHOPPY: The production staff added 4.2 percent more Teflon. This resulted in more density. It also resulted in higher production costs. The process manager evaluated the thicker coating for protective qualities. She found that the Teflon coating was only 10 percent stronger. Costs were 18.4 percent higher. She reduced the Teflon additive to its original level. She kept in mind cost efficiency.

SMOOTH: To increase the density, the production staff added 4.2 percent more Teflon. *Yet* this measure resulted in higher production costs. *After* the process manager evaluated the thicker coating for protective qualities, she found that *it* was 10 percent stronger; *however,* costs were 18.4 percent higher. Keeping in mind cost efficiency, she reduced the Teflon additive to its original level.

ANALYSIS: The original choppy paragraph of eight sentences is rewritten to form a much smoother paragraph of four sentences. The ideas of the original, separate sentences have for the most part been combined in longer structures that make clear the logical relationships between these ideas. Transitional expressions are shown in italics. The main techniques used in the process of revision are illustrated in this book under SUBORDINATION, TRANSITIONS, and VARIETY IN SENTENCE PATTERNS.

coh | COHERENCE

Rewrite the marked passage from scratch.

A passage that lacks coherence simply makes no sense. It is illogical in thought or in organization — and often in both. You probably *think* you know just what you wanted to say, but your message has somehow come out garbled. You have not managed to communicate clearly to the reader, and there are few things more frustrating in the business world than to struggle with an apparently meaningless message.

Coherent writing makes one idea flow naturally and clearly into the next. Relationships between ideas are shown by accurate connectives, such as conjunctions and transitions (see SUBORDINATION and TRANSITIONS). Each part of your developing thought emerges exactly when needed. Important ideas are emphasized, unimportant ideas are de-emphasized, and irrelevant ideas are kept out of the picture.

In rewriting, do not tinker with what you now have on paper. Call to mind your original idea and start writing afresh. Try to express your idea as clearly and as patiently as if you were explaining it to a friend who is hearing the subject for the first time.

EXAMPLE 1 — INCOHERENT BUSINESS LETTER: I sent you a bill for $25. My bill is really $250. Please pay in three installments for your inconvenience, minus what you paid by mistake. It was due back in August but is now due in November. Thank you for your understanding.

This explanation of an incorrect bill is hardly enlightening. How much is owed? What was the cause of the error? Why is the due date changed? The phrase "for your inconvenience" actually insults the reader instead of offering the apology the writer intended. Writers cannot afford to assume that their readers are going to be mind readers. Here is the same incoherent letter completely revised — with more explanatory detail, proper use of connectives, and better organization of ideas to achieve the goal of clarity.

SAME LETTER MADE COHERENT: Because of a typographical error, you were billed for only $25 on your last invoice. Your correct bill is for $250 to cover the purchase of five Style No. 259 draperies last July 6. Since we have already received your payment of

$25, your balance now stands at $225. To show our appreciation of your understanding in this matter, we will be happy to accept your payment of the $225 in three monthly installments of $75 each beginning September 1 and ending November 1. Thank you for your cooperation.

EXAMPLE 2 — INCOHERENT MEMORANDUM: Follow these directions when submitting your report. The introduction necessitates the table of contents when it is not used. Roman numerals outline the sections and subsections handling dividing and organizing such as factors to be considered and recommendations. Provide conclusions, for instance, with reasonableness and practicality in mind as in moving the plant taking into consideration the expense involved.

The problem with the this paragraph is not simply poor punctuation or an impersonal, bureaucratic tone. After the first sentence, the remaining three are incoherent because they are structurally "garbled." Word groups that should function as modifiers of nouns and verbs — especially the clauses and phrases beginning with *when, handling, such as* — do not clearly modify anything earlier in their respective sentences. A thorough revision is required that clears up these sentence-structure problems. Further aids toward clarity are the laying out of directions in the form of a list and the use of parallel verbs in the imperative mood (*use, use, provide*).

SAME MEMORANDUM REVISED: Follow these directions when submitting your report:

1. Use a table of contents or an introduction, but not both, to set forth your ideas.
2. Use Roman-numeral outline form to divide and organize your material into sections and subsections.
3. Provide reasonable and practical conclusions that take into consideration such factors as the expense involved or the long-range effects. For instance, moving the plant might solve some of our transportation problems, but the cost involved would be prohibitive.

: / | COLON

Use a colon to introduce material that is expected to follow, such as a specific explanation or list of items, a formal quotation, or quotations longer than one sentence.

1. COLON INTRODUCING AN EXPLANATION OR LIST

EXPLANATION: Always remember this: Wear your hard hat when you operate the hoist. [When a full sentence follows the colon, capitalize the first word.]

EXPLANATION: The new business lacked one thing: capital.

LIST OF ITEMS: You will need several items to begin the project: paper, tape, glue, and twine.

As follows and *the following* usually signal the need for a colon.

* Study the following carefully before you vote: the minutes of the last meeting, the 1984 fiscal report, and the prospectus for 1985.

CAUTION: A colon comes at the end of an otherwise complete sentence. Do not place a colon between a verb and its object or between a preposition and its object.

WRONG: The trip includes: airfare, hotel, and two meals a day.

REVISED: The trip includes the following: airfare, hotel, and two meals a day.

WRONG: He ordered several new tests such as: a CAT scan, a lung scan, and a stress examination.

REVISED: He ordered several new tests such as a CAT scan, a lung scan, and a stress examination.

2. COLON INTRODUCING A FORMAL QUOTATION

Formal quotations usually consist of official or authoritative statements of some length.

* The mayor stated last night during the press conference: "There will be no tax increase next year if we strictly adhere to the budget proposed at yesterday's meeting."

NOTE: Informal quotations are introduced by a comma: The mayor said, "Thanks for your hospitality."

3. QUOTATIONS LONGER THAN ONE SENTENCE

* To the charge of racial prejudice, the mayor snapped: "Black or white is all the same to me. I am absolutely color-blind!"

comp | COMPARISON

Add the word or words necessary to form a logically complete comparison.

Incomplete or faulty comparisons lead to illogical or ungrammatical statements. (If your error involves the words *better, best, worse,* or *worst,* see ADJECTIVE.)

INCOMPLETE: Detroit is larger than any city in Michigan.
REVISED: Detroit is larger than any *other* city in Michigan. [The use of *other* clearly tells the reader that Detroit is a city in Michigan, not outside it.]

ILLOGICAL: The cursor on the old word processor is faster than the new machine. [This statement compares the cursor to the whole new word processor.]
REVISED: The cursor on the old word processor is faster than *the cursor* on the new machine.

INCOMPLETE: This year IBM grossed at least as much, if not more than, last year. [The complete phrase should be *as much as.*]
REVISED: This year IBM grossed at least as much *as,* if not more than, last year.

---

con | CONVERSATIONAL

Use a conversational, personal style whenever appropriate.

As business becomes more and more automated and impersonal, the human touch in any business transaction becomes much more appreciated. The stiff formality of the business correspondence of several decades ago now sounds insincere and pretentious to most readers. A professional style, however, does not require a stiff and impersonal tone. The conversational touch in your messages not only helps you get your business accomplished but also builds good will. See also SINCERITY.

IMPERSONAL: Should you desire additional orders, avail yourself of the preprinted forms enclosed.
CONVERSATIONAL: When you want to reorder, just use the order forms I have enclosed.

IMPERSONAL: Prior to insertion of the appropriate mailing label, confirm that the postage levers are correctly positioned.
CONVERSATIONAL: Make sure the postage levers are set for the right amount before you insert the mailing label.

NOTE: Some business communications are still very formal occasions. A proposal to merge two companies, a sympathy letter, or an international communication are instances in which a conversational tone might appear to make light of a serious situation.

Strive for a genuine note of professional courtesy.

Courtesy in a business communication means more than just good manners. It means that a genuine warmth of tone and a real desire to be of service should be readily apparent in your letters and memorandums.

Do more than just thank your readers or invite them to call if they have questions. These trite expressions come across as insincere to many people. Instead, think of ways in which you can be genuinely helpful. Include something extra whenever possible in your letters. For instance, if you are confirming hotel reservations to out-of-town guests, enclose a sight-seeing map of the city, mention the entertainment the hotel lounge will be offering the week of their stay, or remind them to bring their warm-up suits because the hotel has its own rooftop jogging track. Once you put yourself in your readers' place and imagine how you would like to be treated in their situation, your business messages will be refreshingly courteous. (See also EASY ACTION and TACT.)

Here is a list of some all-too-common breaches of etiquette in business communications. Avoid these discourtesies if possible:

1. Taking longer than one business week to answer mail. If you cannot answer a letter promptly, at least send an acknowledgment postcard to your reader.
2. Accusing someone else of being responsible for a problem.
3. Exaggerating or deliberately misleading the reader.
4. Using humor or sarcasm in questionable taste. Except in some special kinds of advertising, witticisms tend to fall flat in business correspondence.
5. Refusing to apologize. When you are at fault, immediately admit your mistake and apologize good-naturedly.
6. Phrasing sales communications in a manner that just skirts the truth.
7. Appearing to give orders through the use of phrases such as "you must" or "we require."

Here are some examples of discourteous messages and their courteous counterparts:

DISCOURTEOUS: We are interested in your tinted plexiglass and want you to get your price list to us fast.

COURTEOUS: Your company sells tinted plexiglass that would suit our needs exactly. Please send your price list to me so that an order can be placed right away.

DISCOURTEOUS: We have a new teller who obviously did not know how to enter the interest correctly in your passbook.
COURTEOUS: Sorry — we made a mistake. Your passbook has been adjusted to show the interest your savings earned.

TRITE COURTESY: Should you have any questions, please do not hesitate to call upon us.
COURTEOUS: I'll be calling you in a few days to see if you have any questions.

CS | COMMA SPLICE

Change the comma to a period or semicolon.

A comma splice joins or splices two separate sentences with a comma. If a sentence is a unit of thought, then a comma splice — a type of run-on sentence — blurs the edges between one thought and another.

COMMA SPLICE: Our supplies are running low, I suggest we reorder immediately.
REVISION 1: Our supplies are running low. I suggest we reorder immediately.

Changing the comma to a period keeps two separate thoughts in two separate sentences. But the comma can be changed to a semicolon if the two thoughts are very closely related, as they are in this case. (See SEMICOLON.) Use the semicolon when appropriate, but remember to *use it sparingly.*

REVISION 2: Our supplies are running low; I suggest we reorder immediately.

Comma splices often involve transitional expressions: single words such as *then, thus, therefore, however, consequently;* and phrases such as *in fact, for example, that is,* and *on the other hand.* These common transitions act as logical bridges connecting two thoughts. Their presence signals a new main clause or new sentence.

COMMA SPLICE: First, feed the paper through the printer by releasing the bail lever, then select the character spacing desired.
REVISION 1: First, feed the paper through the printer by releasing the bail lever. Then select the character spacing desired.

Revision 1 changes the comma to a period. However, the semicolon is often the best way to correct errors involving transitional expressions.

REVISION 2: First, feed the paper through the printer by releasing the bail lever; then select the character spacing desired.

COMMA SPLICE: We are very low in clerical support, in fact, one of our best secretaries is leaving next week.

REVISION 1: We are very low in clerical support. In fact, one of our best secretaries is leaving next week.

REVISION 2: We are very low in clerical support; in fact, one of our best secretaries is leaving next week.

NOTE: These examples show the use of the semicolon with transitional expressions that link main clauses. Do not confuse *coordinating conjunctions (and, but, or, nor, for, yet, so)* with transitional expressions. When coordinating conjunctions link two main clauses, place a *comma* before the conjunction. (See COMMA.)

Transitional expressions are not always found at the beginning of a new main clause. They are often found in some other position. Do not assume that a period or semicolon should always appear before a transitional expression:

ERROR [COMMA SPLICE *PLUS* MISPLACED SEMICOLON]: We are very low in clerical support, one of our best secretaries; in fact, is leaving next week.

REVISION 1: We are very low in clerical support. One of our best secretaries, in fact, is leaving next week. [The two main clauses, treated as two sentences, can be separated by a period.]

REVISION 2: We are very low in clerical support; one of our best secretaries, in fact, is leaving next week. [When a transitional expression interrupts a clause — as *in fact* does here — it is set off by commas.]

D I DICTION

Change the marked word or phrase to one that expresses your meaning more exactly or to one that is more appropriate in tone.

1. MEANING

Your *diction* is your choice of words. Consult the glossary of commonly misused words provided in this section. If the glossary does not deal with your problem, consult a large and fairly recent dictionary.

2. TONE

The tone of business writing is most often serious and straightforward. To maintain a consistent tone, avoid abrupt shifts from formal to informal expressions, from layman's vocabulary to technical jargon (see VOCABULARY LEVEL) and vice-versa. Consult a large desk-type dictionary — the more recent the better — for the usage label of a particular word (for example, *slang, informal, technical, nonstandard*). If a word is not labeled, it is *standard* usage, acceptable in a normal business style. Nonstandard (or substandard) vocabulary, such as *ain't, irregardless,* or *nohow,* is not acceptable in business writing because it is frowned upon by virtually all educated speakers and writers. The writer who innocently uses such expressions gives the impression of being illiterate.

GLOSSARY OF COMMONLY MISUSED WORDS

A, an. Use *a* before words beginning with consonant sounds: *a* ledger, *a* word processor. Use *an* before words beginning with vowel sounds (usually represented by the letters *a, e, i, o,* and *u*). Do not, however, confuse vowel *sounds* and *letters.* Write *a union,* not *an union,* because the beginning sound of *union* is *y,* a consonant, not a vowel. Similarly, write *a one-armed bandit,* not *an one-armed bandit,* because *one* begins with the consonant sound *w.*

Adapt, adopt, adept. *To adapt* means *to adjust* or *to change* : I adapt easily to new climates. I have adapted your speech for use in my report. *To adopt* means *to make one's own*: We have adopted new safety procedures. *Adept* is an adjective meaning *highly skilled*: She is adept at typing.

Adverse, averse. *Adverse* means *unfavorable*: He had an adverse reaction to the new drug. To be *averse (to)* is to be *opposed*: I am averse to all such proposals.

Advice, advise. *Advice* is the noun: He ignored her advice. *Advise* is the verb: She advised him to change careers.

Affect, effect. *To affect* is *to change* or *to influence*: How did the layoff affect the economy? The verb *to affect* is often confused with the noun *effect,* meaning *result*: The new policy had no effect (not *affect*) on sales. Less frequently, *to affect* is confused with *to effect,* meaning *to cause or bring about*: The new president has effected (not *affected*) a turnabout in our corporate image.

Aggravate, irritate. *To aggravate* means *to make an already bad situation worse*: Inflation aggravated the already shaky economy. *Aggravate* is often misused for *irritate,* meaning *to annoy*: His know-it-all tone irritated (not *aggravated*) Mr. Wyelittle.

Allusion, illusion. An *allusion* is a *reference to something*: My memo made no allusion to your misconduct. *Illusion* is a *false notion*: Henderson was under the illusion that he got along with everybody.

Alot, a lot. *Alot* is a misspelling for *a lot,* which is an informal phrase. Use such terms as *many, much, very much,* or *great deal,* depending on the context.

Already, all ready. *Already* means *previously*: We already discussed the agenda. Do not confuse *already* with *all ready,* which means *all are completely prepared*: The papers are all ready for signing.

Alright, all right. *Alright* is a misspelling of *all right.*

Altogether, all together. *Altogether* means *entirely*: I am altogether delighted with your success. *All together* means *united in a group*: The letters are all together in your drawer.

Amount, number. *Amount* is often misused for *number.* Use *amount* for a quantity that cannot be counted as the sum of individual parts: They did a great amount of research. Use *number* for a sum of individual, countable items: A large number of factors were each carefully considered.

Anyone, any one. *Anyone* means *any person*: Anyone can learn to write well. *Any one* is used before an *of*-phrase: Any one of the managers could handle this.

Anyway, any way. *Anyway* means *in any case* or *anyhow*: Anyway, Thompson is no longer employed here. *Any way* means *any method*: Is there any way to bring Thompson back?

Anyways. Nonstandard for *anyway.*

Around, about. *Around* means *circling*: Trees were planted around the building. Do not use *around* for *about,* meaning *approximately:* Meet me at about (not *around*) ten o'clock.

At. Do not use after *where*: Where is my book *at*? Correct: Where is my book?

Awhile, a while. *Awhile* is a one-word adverb: I thought *awhile* before acting. It splits into two words after a preposition: I thought *for a while* before acting. Also: *a while* ago, not *awhile* ago.

Badly, bad. After a linking verb, use *bad*: I feel *bad* about his leaving. (See ADJECTIVE.) Use *badly* as an adverb after non-linking verbs: I performed badly on the evaluation.

Because. Do not write *the reason . . . is because.* Write *the reason . . . is that*: The reason I am here is that (not *because*) you invited me.

Being that, seeing that, seeing as. Unacceptable forms for *because* or *since.*

Beside, besides. *Beside* means *next to*: Place the new file cabinet beside the teletype. *Besides* means *in addition to*: Who attended the meeting besides you?

Between, among. *Between* is used for *two* items: The purse was split between the two winners. *Among* is used for *more than two* items: The purse was split among the three top contestants.

Can, may. *Can* expresses ability: *Can* you type 60 wpm? *May* expresses permission (You *may* leave now) or possibility (I *may* still arrive on time).

Capital, capitol. *Capital* is a city in which the governmental offices of a state are located: The capital of Massachusetts is Boston. *Capital* is also the economic value of a company or individual: The firm's capital is valued at $2 million. A *capitol* is *the building* where a state legislature meets: The *Capitol* (capitalized) is the building in which the U.S. Congress assembles in Washington, D.C.

Choose, chose. Do not confuse the present tense *choose* (rhymes with *snooze*) with the past tense *chose* (rhymes with *nose*).

Cite, sight, site. *Cite* means *to mention*: My article was cited in his report. A *sight* is a *special view*: We toured the city and saw the sights. A *site* is a *location*: We have chosen the site of our new building.

Compare to, compare with. You *compare to* when you point out likenesses in things otherwise different: He compared their pizza to cardboard. You *compare with* to find both likenesses and differences in things that are generally similar: After comparing this year's performance standards with last year's, I found last year's inferior.

Complement, compliment. To *complement* means to *go with*: This scarf complements your dress perfectly. To *compliment* is to *praise*: I complimented her on her outfit.

Complementary, complimentary. Do not confuse the technical term complementary (as in *complementary colors*) with *complimentary*, meaning *free*, as in "Please have a complimentary copy of *The Courier*."

Confidant, confident. A *confidant* is a person someone trusts with secrets: He is the manager's confidant. *Confident* means *self-assured*: Sales representatives are usually confident people.

Conscience, conscious. *Conscience* is your sense of right and wrong: Let your conscience be your guide. Conscious means *aware*: She was not conscious of the pickpocket's approach.

Continual, continuous. *Continual* means *at frequent intervals*: There were continual interruptions during the meeting. *Continuous* means *without stopping*: The clatter of the typewriters was continuous.

Council, counsel. *Council* is a committee or government body: The employees' council is sponsoring a picnic. *Counsel* (verb) means *to advise*: I counseled her to take calculus. *Counsel* (noun) means *advice*: This administration needs calm counsel and constructive leadership. *Counsel* also means *attorney*: I was appointed to act as the defendant's counsel.

Elicit, illicit. *Elicit* means *to draw forth*: The poll elicited a wide range of responses. *Illicit* means *illegal*: Illicit acts are grounds for dismissal.

Eminent, imminent. *Eminent* means *distinguished, prominent*: Dr. Sykes is an eminent professor of physics. *Imminent* means *about to happen*: The black clouds signaled an imminent storm.

Equally as. An expression like *equally as good* contains an unnecessary *as*. Write *equally good* or *just as good*.

Except, accept. *Except* is often misused for *accept*. *Except* is a preposition meaning *but*; *accept* is a verb meaning *to receive willingly*: They *accepted* everyone *except* him.

Explicit, implicit. *Explicit* means *openly stated*. Her instructions were explicit: No smoking. *Implicit* means *not openly stated*: His anger was implicit in his abrupt departure.

Fewer, less. Use *fewer* for things you can state in the plural: Fewer employees attended today's seminar than yesterday's. Use *less* for the amount or degree of something you would not make plural: Less waste means more profit.

Formally, formerly. *Formally* means *ceremoniously*: He formally accepted the nomination. *Formerly* means *previously*: Mr. Willette, now retired, was formerly the company president.

Further, farther. *Further* is often loosely used for *farther*. *Farther* is preferred for literal distance: We drove two blocks farther. *Further* is preferred for time and for subjective senses of extension: His explanation got him into further trouble. Let me consider this further.

Good, well. For the distinction between *good* and *well* after a linking verb, see ADJECTIVE.

Healthy, healthful. What *has* health is healthy; what *gives* health is healthful: Florida's healthful climate continues to keep me healthy.

In regards to. Nonstandard for *in regard to.*

Infer, imply. Do not use *infer* when you mean *imply. Infer* is *to draw a conclusion*: From OPEC's recent price reductions we can infer a worldwide oil glut. *Imply* is *to suggest without stating directly*: Her frown implies that she remains unconvinced.

Insure, ensure, assure. *Insure* means *to cover against loss or damage*: Is this building insured against vandalism? *Ensure* is *to make sure of*: To ensure your safety, please fasten your seat belt. *Assure* is *to pledge*: I assured him of our continued support.

Irregardless. Nonstandard for *regardless.*

It's, its. *It's* means *it is*: It's not important. *Its* is the possessive pronoun meaning *belonging to it*: The manual was missing its cover.

Kind of, sort of. These expressions are usually too informal for business writing. Use *somewhat* or *rather.*

Lay, lie. *To lay* is *to set down*. PRESENT TENSE: I *lay* the mail on your desk every day. PAST TENSES: Yesterday I *laid* the mail on your secretary's desk by mistake. Until now I *have* always *laid* your mail in its proper place. *To lie* is *to rest or recline.* PRESENT TENSE: When I *lie* down, I think better. PAST TENSES: Yesterday I *lay* down to think but fell asleep. I suppose I *have lain* down on the job once too often.

Liable, likely. Both express probability, but *liable* suggests negative consequences of an action. You are *likely* to receive the shipment in three or four days. If you do not order now, you are *liable* to miss out on this unusual offer.

Like, as. Do not use *like* (a preposition) for *as* or *as if* (a subordinating conjunction *followed by a subject-verb combination*): WRONG: Do *like* I say. RIGHT: Do *as* I say. WRONG: It looks *like* you have won. RIGHT: It looks *as if* you have won. The preposition *like* means *similar to* and is correctly used as follows: He looks *like me;* there's no place *like home.* (*Me* and *home* are objects of the preposition *like.*)

Loose, lose. *Loose* is a common misspelling of *lose* (pronounced *looz*): I often *lose* (not *loose*) my keys. *Loose,* used correctly, means *not tight.*

Most. Nonstandard for *almost,* which means *nearly.* WRONG: *Most* everyone here agrees with you. RIGHT: *Almost* everyone here agrees with you.

Of. A misspelling of the contraction *'ve* in *could've, may've, might've, would've, should've.* WRONG: He should *of* known better. RIGHT: He should*'ve* known better. BETTER: He should *have* known better. (In general, avoid contractions in a business style.)

Past, passed. *Past* is a preposition (see definition under AGREEMENT) meaning *beyond*: The car drove past the hitchhiker. *Passed* is a verb meaning *went beyond*: The car passed the hitchhiker. *Past,* as a noun, means *an earlier time*: She is a prisoner of the past. *Past,* as an adjective, means *relating to an earlier time*: Your *past* performance indicates success to come.

Personal, personnel. *Personal* means *private*: The letter was marked "Personal." *Personnel* means *persons employed within an organization*: All administrative personnel will meet here on Tuesday.

Perspective, prospective. *Perspective* means *viewpoint*: From her perspective, the statement was true. *Prospective* means *likely*: Treat prospective clients with utmost courtesy.

Precede, proceed. *Precede* means *to go ahead of*: A 200-word abstract precedes the body of the article. *Proceed* means *to continue*: You may proceed with your analysis.

Principal, principle. *Principal,* as a noun, means *head of a school* or *a sum of money.* The principal handed me my diploma. If I spend my principal, I will have nothing left to earn interest on. *Principal,* as an adjective, means *primary*.Drunken driving is the principal cause of teen-age car accidents. A *principle* (noun) is a *rule* or *guideline*: How do we put these high-sounding principles into practice?

Raise, rise. *Raise* means *to lift or push up:* He tried to raise his grades. *Rise* means *to go up:* The sun rises every morning.

Real. Do not misuse as an adverb, as in *real good, real well.* See ADVERB.

Reason is because. See BECAUSE.

Regards. See IN REGARDS TO.

Seeing as, seeing that. See BEING THAT.

—self. Use *himself, herself, myself, themselves,* etc., for emphasis, not when a simple pronoun will do. WRONG: Either John or *myself* will enter the data. RIGHT: Either John or *I* will enter the data. CORRECT USE OF *MYSELF* FOR EMPHASIS: I entered the data myself.

So. 1. Frequent use of the coordinating conjunction *so* leads to an informal, loose style. Correct this habit through SUBORDINATION. 2. Do not use *so* as a short form of the subordinating conjunction *so that*: I worked late yesterday so that (not *so*) we could leave early today. 3. Do not use *so* in formal writing as an intensifier. INFORMAL: We were *so* happy to hear from you. FORMAL: We were *very* (or *extremely*) happy to hear from you.

Sometime, some time. If you mean *an indefinite "point" in the future,* use *sometime*: Stop over sometime during a coffee break. If you mean *an indefinite "amount" of time,* use *some time*: We spent some time shopping.

Stationary, stationery. *Stationary* means *immovable; stationery* means *writing supplies.*

Strata, stratum. *Strata* is a plural and takes a plural verb: All *strata* of society *are* represented by our organization. *Stratum,* the singular, takes a singular verb: Every *stratum* of society *is* represented by our organization.

Sure. Do not misuse as an adverb. WRONG: I am *sure* glad. See ADVERB.

Their, there, they're. *Their* is the possessive pronoun meaning *belonging to them*: Their profits were eaten up by taxes. *There* is an adverb of place: I went there by myself. *There* is also an introductory word (*there is, there are*): There is no cause for alarm. *They're* is the contraction of *they are*: They're biting off more than they can chew.

Then, than. *Then* is an adverb of time: He added the figures by hand, then rechecked them with the calculator. *Than* is used in comparisons: She adds faster than Jim.

Thru. Unacceptable misspelling for *through,* except in *thruway.*

To, too. The preposition *to* (*to* the store, *to* all intents and purposes) is commonly misspelled as the adverb *too,* meaning *also* (She, too, is a power in the organization) or *excessively* (The coffee is too hot).

Try and. In a formal style, use *try to*: Please try to (not *try and*) adjust gracefully to this change in hours.

Waiver, waver. A *waiver* (noun) is *a legal statement granting an exception to the rule*: She signed a waiver, giving up her right to read the letters in her file. To *waver* (verb) means *to hesitate*: Harold wavers when it comes down to making hard decisions.

Which, who. Use *which* to refer to animals and things: I know which copier is better. Use *who* to refer to people: Edwards is the attorney who won our case for us.

While. Do not use the conjunction *while* in place of *but* or *whereas*: Whereas (not *While*) I enjoy lazy vacations, my colleague enjoys adventurous ones.

Who, whom. *Who* is a relative pronoun acting as the subject: He found out who allowed the shipment to be sent c.o.d. [*Who* is the subject of the verb *allowed.*] *Whom* is a relative pronoun acting as the object: Mrs. Genovese understood whom I meant. [*Whom* is the direct object of the verb *meant.*] See CASE.

Who's, whose. *Who's* is the contraction of *who is*: Who's minding the store? *Whose* is the possessive pronoun meaning *belonging to whom*: "Whose woods these are, I think I know."

Your, you're. *Your* is a possessive pronoun meaning *belonging to you*: Here is your hat. *You're* is the contraction of *you are*: You're sure to be pleased with the results. (Avoid contractions in a formal business style.)

dang | DANGLING MODIFIER

1. Revise the element marked as *dangling* by changing it into a subordinate clause.
2. Revise the main clause. Make the subject of the main clause the logical word for the dangling element to modify.

Modifiers dangle when they have nothing in the sentence to modify or when they grammatically appear to modify an absurd or illogical subject.

DANGLER: *Walking across the street,* the office came into view. [Who is walking? The missing *person* walking is the logical word for the dangling phrase to modify, but that logical word does not appear in the sentence. Instead, *the office* appears to be walking.]

REVISION 1: *As I walked across the street,* the office came into view. [The dangling modifier is changed into a subordinate clause, a group of words beginning with a subordinating conjunction — *As* — followed by a subject — *I* — and a verb — *walked.*]

REVISION 2: Walking across the street, *I saw the office.* [The modifier *Walking across the street* is not changed. Instead, the main clause is recast. Now, *Walking* logically modifies the subject of the main clause, *I.*]

DANGLER: *To write well,* your dictionary should be at your side. [Will the dictionary do the writing?]

REVISION 1: *If you want to write well,* your dictionary should be at your side.

REVISION 2: To write well, *you should keep your dictionary at your side.*

---

dash [—] DASH

Insert a dash, or remove an improperly used one.

A dash is an informal punctuation mark that sets off an interrupting element in a sentence. Do not use a dash (or pair of dashes) where commas, colons, or parentheses would be the normal punctuation. Except under special circumstances, business writing avoids the use of dashes. Most keyboards do not have a dash key. When you do use a dash, type it with two hyphen strokes: *Inflationary?--No!*

1. DASH WITH COMMAS

Use a dash to set off an interrupting element when commas are already used.

- Agendas, note pads, pencils, calculators — all the thinking tools were supplied at the seminar. [Another comma after *calculators* might suggest that another item in the series was coming.]

2. DASH FOR EMPHASIS

Use a dash, not parentheses or commas, to give emphasis to an interrupting element. Compare the following sentences:

- Several states (mainly those in the Midwest) lobbied against the grain embargo. [The parentheses muffle the interrupting element and make it appear unimportant.]

- Several states, mainly those in the Midwest, lobbied against the grain embargo. [Set off by commas, the interrupting element now gains more emphasis.]

- Several states — mainly those in the Midwest — lobbied against the grain embargo. [In this sentence the interrupting element receives the most emphasis. Dashes are stronger stress marks than either parentheses or commas.]

doc I DOCUMENTATION

Give credit to your source whenever you borrow material.

Authors have a property right to their own ideas as well as to their manner of expressing them. Their ideas are the products of their personal inventiveness, and their manner of expressing them results from a long process of apprenticeship to the art of writing. Because their reputations and incomes depend on exclusive marketing rights to their words and ideas, authors' rights are protected by law. When you use the specific words or ideas of another person in your own writing and you fail to mention whose they are, you suggest that you personally are taking credit for that material. Such misrepresentation is a form of theft called *plagiarism*, and plagiarists are liable to legal prosecution.

DOCUMENTATION PROCEDURES

Whenever you borrow another person's original material, acknowledge your source by documenting it. In formal business writing, documentation usually involves two procedures — the inclusion of *notes* and a *bibliography*. The use of notes involves two steps:

1. In your own text place a superscript [1] immediately at the end of the first item you have borrowed, a superscript [2] after the second item, and so on.

2. Enter a correspondingly numbered *footnote* at the bottom of the same page or a note in a separate section of "Notes" at the end of your report, where all notes are presented in numerical order. A full note or footnote includes precise information specifying the author, title, place of publication, publisher, date of publication, and page number(s), *in that order.*

EXAMPLE OF FOOTNOTING PROCEDURE:

> The forming of partnerships as a way of doing business will always have appeal. Two or more individuals can join forces for more capital to invest, more skills to offer in the market, and more security in case of hard times. The big disadvantage, however, is that "each partner is individually liable to creditors for debts incurred by the partnership."[1]

---

[1]Philip E. Fess and C. Rollin Niswonger, *Accounting Principles,* 13th ed. (Cincinnati: South-Western, 1981), p. 388.

The second procedure generally followed is to include a "Bibliography" section at the end of your report. (If you have a section headed "Notes," the bibliography section follows it.) The bibliography lists, in alphabetical order, all the sources consulted, whether they appear in notes or footnotes or not. Compare the footnote form with the slightly different bibliography format for the same book. Note that page references are omitted.

> Fess, Philip E. and Niswonger, C. Rollin. *Accounting Principles.* 13th
> ed. Cincinnati: South-Western, 1981.

Formal versus informal documentation.

The previous procedures represent the formal way of documenting sources. The style of note and bibliography entries has become traditional, so that magazine articles, lectures, pamphlets, volumes of a work, reprints, anonymous works, and many other possible sources all require their own format. A detailed discussion of footnote and bibliography format is beyond the scope of this book, but you may consult a term-paper or library-paper reference book such as *Research Papers,* sixth edition, by William Coyle (Indianapolis: Bobbs-Merrill Educational Publishing, 1985).

For less formal writing, any honest effort to credit the author of your material is usually acceptable. For example, documentation can often be included in the sentence itself, as in the italicized portion of the following:

• *At yesterday's meeting Mr. Collins said,* "A $10,000 increase in the manufacturing budget is not possible until March."

Knowing when to document.

Knowing *how* to document something is largely a mechanical matter involving the use of the proper format conventions. More often, a writer faces the problem of knowing *when* to document. Here are some guidelines to help you:

1. Do not document a statistic or fact that is generally available in encyclopedias or other reference works. For instance, you could take from an encyclopedia, without having to use a footnote, the fact that the first completely electronic computer was invented in 1946 by John Mauchly and John Eckert, Jr. If you borrow the exact wording of your source, however, you must quote as well as document.

2. If you quote someone's exact words, whether or not the ideas or facts are generally available, you must document the source.

3. When you change only the phrasing but keep the content and organization of the materials the same, you are *paraphrasing.* The paraphrased passage requires a note (or footnote) and a bibliography entry in a formal paper and acknowledgment of some kind in an informal one. Paraphrasing is documented like any quotation, but you do not use quotation marks. Remember,

though, that paraphrasing is not simply the substitution of synonyms for the author's original words. It involves a thorough restating of the author's idea in your own words and sentence structure.

4. If you are unsure whether you are plagiarizing, play it safe: *when in doubt, document!*

Make it easy for readers to do what you ask.

In communications that aim to persuade, you increase your chances of getting the desired result if you make it as convenient as possible for readers to act as you wish them to. The idea behind *easy action* is not only convenience for readers; it is also the attempt to spur them into immediate action. Every sales communication should end with some specific request for action from readers before the interest you have aroused in them has a chance to wane.

Here are several ways of designing your correspondence to increase the level of favorable and early response you desire from your readers:

1. Include printed order forms, catalogs, price lists, or specifications.
2. Include coupons, complimentary offers, or free samples.
3. Enclose addressed envelopes — with postage, if possible.
4. Enclose free parking tickets if appropriate, especially if your business is located in a busy downtown area.
5. Enclose directions or a map to your place of business.
6. Offer a toll-free 800 number for information or ordering.
7. Offer to visit readers with literature and samples, and to give demonstrations.
8. Offer the convenience of credit-card purchasing.
9. Offer delivery or pick-up or shop-at-home service.
10. Mention your business hours, especially any evening hours you may have.
11. Mention alternate phone numbers in case the line is busy.
12. Invite readers to call you for a tour of your facilities.

In business writing use an ellipsis — three double-spaced periods (. . .)— to indicate that you have intentionally left something out of quoted material.

ORIGINAL, UNCUT VERSION: The proposal offers several alternatives, a loan, a cutback, a price increase, and various reductions in personnel; none, however, provides an adequate solution.

SHORTENED VERSION WITH ELLIPSIS: The proposal offers several alternatives, a loan, a cutback, . . . ; none, however, provides an adequate solution. [Note that the comma and semicolon on either side of the ellipsis are a part of the quoted text.]

When you omit material at the end of a sentence, add a fourth period to serve as the closing mark:

• The proposal offers several alternatives. . . . We have rejected them all.

When omitting one or more paragraphs from your source, use a full line of periods to indicate this major omission:

> Arrangements for your trip from Boston to Los Angeles are confirmed.
>
> . . . .
>
> Your itinerary comes to $780. Please make your check payable to this agency. The deadline for payment is April 22. If we receive your payment by that date, we will have time to cut your tickets and mail them to you. [Note that when you quote whole paragraphs, you do not use quotation marks. Instead, use a short line length and single spacing.]

In advertising copy only, an ellipsis is often used to emphasize material:

• Advanced Formula FloorSheen . . . cuts through grease . . . leaves a durable shine . . . makes you proud of your floors.

---

em | EMPHASIS

Emphasize the more important parts of your message — whether a word, a phrase, or an idea.

Use these techniques:

1. Place important elements at the beginning or end of your sentence, para-

graph, memo, or letter. The most emphatic position is at the end. Emphatic also, but less so, is the beginning. These are positions of stress because they are the most readily remembered parts of a message.

POOR EMPHASIS: The meeting came to an abrupt end because the section head was called away to see about the doughnuts, juice, and coffee for the morning break.

BETTER EMPHASIS: Because the section head was called away to see about the doughnuts, juice, and coffee for the morning break, the meeting came to an abrupt end. [If the main idea is the abrupt ending of the meeting, then it should be placed in the emphatic final position of the sentence.]

2. Change verbs in the passive voice to the more emphatic active voice.

PASSIVE: The sales letters were typed by the five secretaries in record time. [In this example of a sentence cast in the passive voice, the subject, *sales letters,* does not act but instead receives the action of typing; and a form of the verb *be* must come before the verb, *were* typed. In the passive voice, the doer of the action often appears in a minor sentence position, inside a prepositional phrase beginning with *by.* See AGREEMENT, RULE 1 for definition of a prepositional phrase.]

ACTIVE: The five secretaries typed the sales letters in record time. [Now, in the active voice, the doer of the action of the previous sentence, *the five secretaries* — becomes the actual grammatical subject. The indirect *be* form of the verb disappears also.]

3. Repeat key words or grammatical structures for emphasis.

KEY WORDS: She was an *efficient* secretary, but she made an even more *efficient* director of advertising.

GRAMMATICAL STRUCTURES: Without capital, but with unswerving determination, she built a successful business. [The similar prepositional phrases at the beginning emphasize important ideas.]

See also REPETITION and PARALLELISM.

! / | EXCLAMATION POINT

Remove or insert an exclamation point.

Use an exclamation point after any sentence element that is expressed with strong feeling, whether a full sentence or not. Most business correspondence, however, avoids the exclamation point except in advertising copy or sales communications.

PROPER USE: Hurry! The 30-percent-off Royal Linen sale will last only three days.

PROPER USE: Our new Bolton Bank savings certificates earn 13½ percent compound interest — guaranteed!

PROPER USE: Oh, no! Did your drain cleaner let you down again?

Do not clutter your writing with exclamation points. If you stress everything, you wind up stressing nothing because nothing then stands out.

OVERUSED: Greystone Pharmacy is now offering photocopying services! And what a deal! For one nickel you get a crystal-clear copy on high-quality paper! This service is available during our entire business day!

REVISED: Greystone Pharmacy is now offering photocopying services. And what a deal! For one nickel you get a crystal-clear copy on high-quality paper. This service is available during our entire business day.

Never use more than one exclamation point as an end mark.

OVERUSED: 50 percent off!!!
REVISED: 50 percent off!

Use an attractive physical layout — or page format — to enhance the effectiveness of your communication.

Take advantage of the paper that your letter or report is printed on. Think of the blank space as part of the message. Use it to break up large blocks of material that offer little relief to the eye of the reader.

Remember that the visual impact of your communication is the first thing that affects a reader. Psychologically, format can have significant effect on the attitude with which your message is received. Readers want messages to look "easy to take." They want frequent places for the eye and mind to pause. They want clear markers that instantly signal the content and organization of your material. For example, complicated technical information is much more digestible when you use fairly large type; brief, numerous paragraphs; headings denoting divisions of the main subject; and lots of white space. Similarly, keep in mind the layout of an effective résumé: the logical divisions of material marked by clear headings and the generous use of blank areas between relatively short blocks of print. Because employers usually skim a résumé rather than read it in detail, the information on it should be arranged visually so that the most important items are bound to catch the quickly scanning eye.

Here are some helpful format suggestions for all business communications:

1. Use numbers, letters, or dots before each item in a long list. (This list is an example.)
2. Indent minor items to distinguish them visually from major sections.

3. Use a consistent style of type to distinguish headings from subheadings; for example, all main headings in capital letters, all subheadings in italics.

4. Use outlines, charts, or graphs when you have numerous points to make.

5. Use columns when vertical arrangements of information are most practical and visually effective.

6. Use generous margins on all four sides of a sheet.

7. Use half-sheets for brief messages that might lose emphasis on a full page.

frag | FRAGMENTARY SENTENCE

Turn your fragment of a sentence into a complete sentence.

A fragmentary sentence begins with a capital letter and ends with a period, like a sentence — but it lacks at least one element essential to a complete sentence. A fragment, when read aloud, makes no sense as a complete statement. It can often be attached to the previous or following group of words, the main part of the sentence to which it actually belongs. (If it cannot be attached, then it must be rewritten as a complete sentence in itself or rewritten until it can be attached smoothly to the sentence before or after it.)

The heart of a sentence is a subject-verb pattern. If a group of words lacks either a subject or a verb, or both, it is a fragmentary sentence. The exception is the subordinate clause (see the example that follows), which is a fragment even though it has a subject and verb. Here are examples of common types of fragments. The fragments are in italics.

PHRASE FRAGMENTS

ERROR: Our latest computer has an automatic retrieval switch. *In case of accidental erasure of the memory.*
CORRECTED: Our latest computer has an automatic retrieval switch in case of accidental erasure of the memory.

ERROR: The sales manager worked incredibly hard. *Just as hard as the people in the field.*
CORRECTED: The sales manager worked incredibly hard, just as hard as the people in the field.

APPOSITIVE FRAGMENTS

ERROR: We plan to relocate the plant to southern Georgia. *A state whose low energy costs should enable our profits to increase by 12 percent.* [An appositive is a noun or pronoun — *state,* in this example — often with attached modifiers — *whose low energy costs* — that explains or amplifies the noun or pronoun just before it — *Georgia.*]

CORRECTED: We plan to relocate the plant to southern Georgia, a state whose low energy costs should enable our profits to increase by 12 percent.

ERROR: An analysis of company strategies to widen the market in roofing fabrication is needed. *One that will cover both labor and management objectives.*

CORRECTED: An analysis of company strategies to widen the market in roofing fabrication is needed, one that will cover both labor and management objectives.

SUBORDINATE-CLAUSE FRAGMENTS

ERROR: The two-color offset produces a much more attractive print. *As you can see from this sample.* [Although the subordinate clause has a subject and verb — *you can see* — it cannot stand alone as a complete thought, because it begins with a subordinating conjunction — *After.* Reread the subordinate clause in this example by itself. Notice how unfinished it sounds. See also SUBORDINATION.]

CORRECTED: The two-color offset produces a much more attractive print, as you can see from this sample.

ERROR: You may wish to buy a personal computer. *After you find out all the different things it can do.*

CORRECTED: You may wish to buy a personal computer after you find out all the different things it can do.

ACCEPTABLE USE OF FRAGMENTS

In certain types of advertising and sales letters, fragmentary sentences are used intentionally. The purpose may be to create emphasis, produce pauses, or otherwise engage reader attention. Such fragments are acceptable in this kind of writing only *if* they clearly aid in communication.

* Do you want a brighter, whiter smile? *Right away? Of course!*

* A recent-release videotape movie rents for $4 at our tape club. *Just $4! No deposit required. Two full days before return.*

hy [-] | HYPHEN

Insert a hyphen where needed.

Do not confuse a hyphen [-] with a dash [—]. A hyphen connects or divides words; a dash is an informal substitute for a comma, a colon, or parentheses (see DASH).

The five main uses of the hyphen are as follows:

1. to divide words at the end of a line
2. to join numbers between twenty and one hundred
3. to join words that form a single unit of meaning
4. to join words used as a single modifier before a noun
5. to prevent confusion

1. USE A HYPHEN FOR END-OF-LINE WORD DIVISION.

Whenever possible, avoid dividing words. If you have to divide words, divide them only at syllable breaks. Consult a good dictionary when in doubt: *proof-read,* not *proo-fread; produc-tion,* not *prod-uction.*

For typing business correspondence, consult the following specific rules for word division:

a. Do not divide any word less than seven letters long: *into, beyond.*

b. Do not divide proper names, contractions, or figures: *Arthur, haven't, 346,700.*

c. Do not divide words at the ends of more than *two* lines in a row.

d. Do not divide the last word on a page.

e. Do not divide a word so that just one letter is left on the first line (*u-nique*) or so that just two letters are left on the next line (*careful-ly*).

f. Do not divide two vowels unless they are pronounced as two separate sounds as in the following: *appropri-ate, courte-ous.* Wrong: *bre-ak, dismo-unting.*

g. Do not divide words that are pronounced as one syllable: *stopped.*

h. Divide a word containing a hyphen only at the hyphen: *self-discipline,* not *self-discip-line.*

i. Divide compound words where the two words are joined: *black-board.*

j. Divide between double consonants (*fol-low, ambas-sador*) but not if one of the consonants would be detached from the root word (*fall-ing* not *fal-ling*).

k. Divide after a prefix: *pro-duction, re-align.*

l. Divide before a suffix: *announce-ment, immov-able.* If you have a choice, divide before a suffix rather than after a prefix.

m. When a word contains a vowel that is itself a whole syllable (crit • i • cize), divide *after* that vowel: *criti-cize.*

2. USE A HYPHEN FOR NUMBERS BETWEEN TWENTY AND ONE HUNDRED:

* A check for two thousand five hundred *forty-five* dollars.

3. USE A HYPHEN TO JOIN THE PARTS OF CERTAIN COMPOUND NOUNS:

* mock-up, run-through, battle-ax, policy-making

Unfortunately, the use of hyphens in compound nouns is simply a matter of tradition. Some compounds are hyphenated (*mother-in-law, self-esteem*); others have no hyphens (*port of entry, editor in chief*); and still others are joined (*checkbook, typewriter*). Consult an up-to-date dictionary to be sure.

NOTE: Hyphenate nouns with the prefixes or suffixes *self, ex, vice,* and *elect: self-respect, ex-wife, vice-president-elect.*

4. USE A HYPHEN TO JOIN WORDS USED AS A SINGLE MODIFIER BEFORE A NOUN:

* a *high-pressure* salesman
* a *three-week* vacation
* a *well-written* report
* a *two-thirds* majority
* personnel assigned to *four-, six-,* and *eight-hour* shifts [hyphens in a suspended series before a noun]

NOTE: A hyphenated modifier before a noun is not usually hyphenated in other positions.

* The paper was *well written.*
* The shifts are *four, six,* and *eight hours* long.

FURTHER CAUTIONS: Hyphenate fractions in *all* sentence positions: *Three-fourths* of the vote went to Dixon even though she needed no more than a *two-thirds* majority.
   Do not hyphenate an adverb ending in –*ly*: a *clearly written* report, a *sadly misunderstood* message

5. USE A HYPHEN TO PREVENT CONFUSION:

* A small-appliance store [where small appliances are sold]
* A small appliance store [a small store for appliances]
* A re-covered couch [re-upholstered]
* A recovered couch [lost but now found]

Supply the missing word(s) to complete the indicated construction.

PREPOSITION OMITTED: She was very interested and enthusiastic about the report.
REVISED: She was very interested *in* and enthusiastic about the report.

VERB OMITTED: Mr. Egan is the best man we got.
REVISED: Mr. Egan is the best man we've got.
BETTER: Mr. Egan is the best man we have. [In business writing, try to avoid contractions.]

VERB OMITTED: The statistical survey was finished and all the introductory materials typed.
REVISED: The statistical survey was finished and all the introductory materials *were* typed.

PRONOUN OMITTED: I would appreciate if you would call my office.
REVISED: I would appreciate *it* if you would call my office.
BETTER: I would appreciate your calling my office. [This version is less awkward.]

irr | IRRELEVANT

Omit unnecessary information.

In business communications, wasted words are wasted money. Do not pad your writing with irrelevant material. Maintain the impact and unity of your messages by sticking to your point. Say what is essential, but shun long explanations, overly detailed background material — and even excess courtesy. (Thank the reader once, not two or three times. See COURTESY.) To correct a passage marked "irrelevant," just rewrite it to eliminate unnecessary information. Remember that your readers appreciate a brief, clear, uncluttered message — a message that shows respect for the importance of their time. (See also REPETITION and WORDINESS.)

PASSAGE CONTAINING IRRELEVANT MATERIAL: As you recall, last month I asked you to let me know about any accounting jobs available in the West Palm Beach area of Florida. I was talking to a neighbor of mine the other day, and he said the jobs there are relatively low paid. So I have reconsidered and now would like you to refer to me any positions in the Atlanta area. I hear this section offers high salaries and a low cost of living. I also believe Georgia has slightly cooler summers. I am concerned that the heat will really bother me in Florida since I am not used to it. Just give me a call if you hear of anything.

SAME PASSAGE REVISED: As you recall, last month I asked you to let me know about any accounting jobs available in the West Palm Beach area of Florida. Since then I have reconsidered and now feel I would prefer the Atlanta, Georgia, area. Please call me if you hear of any jobs available in this part of the country. [The personal considerations in the original version are irrelevant to the request.]

PASSAGE CONTAINING IRRELEVANT MATERIAL: This word processor allows you to produce error-free correspondence at the touch of a few buttons. With commands such as *delete, insert, block,* and *move,* you can correct mistakes, move whole paragraphs to different positions, and key in changes right over the original text. The terminal screen comes in black with green letters or black with white letters. For flawless letters with the greatest of ease, call one of our sales representatives today.

SAME PASSAGE REVISED: This word processor allows you to produce error-free correspondence at the touch of a few buttons. With commands such as *delete, insert, block,* and *move,* you can correct mistakes, move whole paragraphs to different positions, and key-in changes right over the original text. For flawless letters with the greatest of ease, call one of our sales representatives today. [Information in the original version about the terminal screen is irrelevant to the main idea — producing error-free copy.]

---

ital | ITALICS

Underline the marked word or words.

Italics or slanted type *such as this* is used in printed matter to give unusual emphasis to certain kinds of expressions. If your typewriter can not produce italics, use underlining instead. Never both underline and italicize the same words. Remember, also, not to leave spaces between words when underlining: Gone with the Wind, not Gone with the Wind.

There are five situations that call for italicizing or underlining.

1. Italicize the following types of titles or proper names:

   a. Books: *Encyclopedia Britannica*

   b. Magazines: *Popular Science*

   c. Newspapers: *Times Literary Supplement*

   d. Plays: *South Pacific*

   e. Movies: *Star Wars*

   f. Operas: *La Bohème*

   g. Long poems: *Paradise Lost*

   h. Pamphlets: *Starting Your Own Business*

   i. Paintings: *Master Hare*

   j. Pieces of sculpture: Rodin's *The Thinker*

k. Ships: *S.S. Mardi Gras*

l. Trains: *Red Chief,* but not Amtrak

m. Airplanes: *Spirit of St. Louis,* but not DC 10

n. Spacecraft: *Columbia*

2. Italicize foreign expressions not commonly used in English: *sub rosa* (secretly), *joie de vivre* (keen enjoyment of life), *inter alia* (among other things). Foreign expressions that have achieved general recognition and acceptance in English are no longer italicized: alma mater, per diem, carte blanche.

3. Italicize terms to be defined: The term *FRS* stands for Federal Reserve System.

4. Italicize words, letters, and figures referred to as such, and not for their meaning:

* The report contains too many *ifs.*

* The *c*'s in your handwriting look like *O*'s.

5. Italicize, sparingly, words intended to have strong emphasis: Ms. Shaw wants the income statement *today*

---

log | LOGIC

Rewrite the marked passage to eliminate illogical phrasing or reasoning.

Logic involves the coherent and convincing development of your ideas. A communication that is patterned logically omits no essential piece of information and no necessary step in the writer's argument. Although many types of advertising try to persuade the public through an appeal to emotion rather than logic, the vast majority of business communications depend on a basic respect for logic if they are to be effective. Major financial decisions often depend on a soundly argued, factually solid report. The argumentative force of any piece of writing may be undermined by either illogical phrasing or illogical thinking. When the logic of a passage appears questionable, a careful writer will rethink each step of the argument and rewrite the passage completely.

Illogical statements are often due to *writing* problems such as lack of COHERENCE, INCOMPLETE CONSTRUCTION, MIXED CONSTRUCTION, poor PARAGRAPH structure, a SHIFT IN POINT OF VIEW, ineffective use of TRANSITIONS, or VAGUENESS (all of which are treated in this book). But if your line of *reasoning,* and not your phrasing, is at fault, your communication may be the victim of one of the following very common problems in logic.

1. OVERSIMPLIFICATION
You oversimplify when you assert that something is true but

1. give no evidence to support your claim
2. give inadequate evidence
3. offer too slim or unconvincing an argument

The most persuasive communications provide *adequate evidence* (relevant examples and information) and *sound reasoning* (attention to the multiple facets of a complicated issue). If your assertion is essentially *untrue* and can in no way be supported by the limited evidence or explanation you offer, you have made a *faulty inference*.

EVIDENCE MISSING: Labor-management relations at G. Foster & Sons Millwrights, Inc., are hostile. A walkout is imminent. [We need more evidence than the mere fact of hostile relations to be convinced of a forthcoming strike.]

EVIDENCE PROVIDED: Labor-management relations at G. Foster & Sons Millwrights, Inc., are hostile right now. Last week an employee representative submitted a list of seven demands, but Vice-President Hale rejected them all as "unacceptable." By an informal count made a few days ago, about 45 percent of the employees said they were willing to walk out. Now that management has refused to negotiate any further, it is assumed that a large majority of employees will vote to strike at their meeting two days from now.

FAULTY INFERENCE: Mr. Williams purchases all our solder from high-priced United Welding Supply Company. He must be getting a kickback. [The inference of a kickback is based on very slim evidence.]

CORRECTED: Mr. Williams purchases all our solder from United Welding Supply Company. He feels that even though its prices are a bit higher than most, the pure quality of the solder results in better transistor connections.

2. OVERGENERALIZATION
You overgeneralize when you ignore facts that contradict or otherwise fail to support the *rule* you wish to set up. In mathematics and the sciences, it is possible to find absolute rules that admit no exceptions, but with people it is hard to imagine *any* rule that will prove absolutely true at all times and under all conditions. Learn to "hedge" or qualify your assertions. When appropriate, use words such as *some, many,* or *most* rather than *all;* use *rarely* rather than *never;* or put a safe *practically* or *almost* in front of words such as *always, never, all,* or *none.*

OVERGENERALIZED: Food distributors are interested in marketing the poorest quality food the public will uncomplainingly accept. [Note that *Food distributors* here means "*all* food distributors."]

QUALIFIED: Some food distributors are interested in marketing the poorest quality food the public will uncomplainingly accept.

3. APPEAL TO AUTHORITY

A true expert's opinion is certainly valuable in an argument, but do not rely on false authorities. A Superbowl quarterback is not necessarily the best authority on which aftershave lotion to use. But what about reliance on *genuine* authorities? Do we always *know* who the genuine authorities are? The problem is that even authorities are often found contradicting one another. In addition, new research is always forcing the experts to change their opinions. Whenever possible, therefore, avoid reliance on authorities or authorities alone, and try to support your claims with objective evidence.

DUBIOUS AUTHORITY: The president of the Home Builders' Association said that interest rates for housing mortgages will go down in June. [The "authority" in this case may be somewhat biased.]

IMPROVED: A spokesperson for the Federal Reserve System said that the recent lowering of the prime interest rate should result in a lowering of the home mortgage rate by this June. [A more objective authority — and an objective piece of evidence — are now offered in support of the claim about lower rates to come.]

4. APPEAL TO EMOTION

Emotional appeals are often more convincing than logical arguments. Charity drives depend on such appeals, and many types of advertising, of course, are designed to reach you through your emotions rather than your reason. In most business communications, however, if you appeal to readers' prejudices, fears, and vanities and fail to provide meaningful evidence for your opinions, you risk insulting the intelligence of those readers. If you do state the facts but cannot help throwing in your own opinions, you often produce *slanted statements* that will also offend any intelligent reader.

PREJUDICED STATEMENT: Be sure to live in the right neighborhood. A condominium at Laurel Ridge is on the city's prestigious west side. [The writer's prejudice will insult many dwellers on the east, north, and south sides.]

IMPROVED: Luxurious Laurel Ridge condominiums face the park on the city's west side. They offer 2½ baths, a skylight over the foyer, a fireplace in the master bedroom, and a sunken marble tub in every townhouse model. [This version gives objective evidence of quality and an objective reason — living near the park — to prefer the west side.]

SLANTED STATEMENT: This rather boring and long-winded article attempts to describe the latest innovations in LASER survey equipment.

IMPROVED: This article describes the latest innovations in LASER survey equipment.

5. NON SEQUITUR

Non sequitur is Latin for *it does not follow.* A non sequitur is a statement that does not follow from what was said before. Usually, the problem is that at least one logical step — some necessary bridge or transition between thoughts — has been omitted from the argument:

NON SEQUITUR: Because Child's Closet wants to maintain the lowest prices possible, we do not give refunds.

IMPROVED: Child's Closet wants to maintain the lowest prices possible, but if we give refunds, we wind up taking losses on unsalable returns, costs that must be passed on to our customers. We therefore do not give refunds.

mm I MISPLACED MODIFIER

Place the marked word or group of words closer to the specific word it modifies.

A *modifier* is any word or group of words that gives information about, or *modifies,* another word. These words or word groups are *adjectives* if they modify nouns or pronouns. They are *adverbs* if they modify either verbs, adjectives, or other adverbs.

- The *green* file is *thick*. [*Green* and *thick* are adjectives modifying the noun *file*.]
- The green file is *very* thick. [*Very* is an adverb modifying the adjective *thick*.]
- The green file *of personnel records* fell *from my desk*. [*Of personnel records* is a phrase that acts as a single adjective modifying the noun *file*; *from my desk* is a phrase that acts as a single adverb modifying the verb *fell*.]
- *Falling from my desk,* the green file *that I had carefully assembled* scattered its contents *all over the floor*. [*Falling from my desk* is a participial phrase — a phrase beginning with a present participle, *falling* — that acts as a single adjective modifying the noun *file*, just as *green* does. *That I had carefully assembled* is a relative clause — a clause beginning with the relative pronoun *that* — which also acts as a single adjective and modifies the noun *file*. *All over the floor* is a phrase used as an adverb because it modifies the verb *scattered*.)

PLACING MODIFIERS

A modifier is misplaced when it is too far away from the word it modifies. Sometimes it occurs too close to another that it misleadingly appears to modify. Misplaced modifiers often cause a reader to misunderstand the meaning of a sentence. As a general rule, place all modifiers as close as possible to the words they modify.

MISPLACED: I have just read an article describing how several hard-hit computer companies are managing to stay afloat *in today's paper*.

REVISED: I have just read an article *in today's paper* describing how several hard-hit computer companies are managing to stay afloat.

MISPLACED: She came across the most interesting of the job applicants *flipping through her private interview notes*. [The error here makes it possible to misunderstand the thought entirely.]

REVISED: *Flipping through her private interview notes,* she came across the most interesting of the job applicants. [Now that the participial modifier is placed close to the word it modifies, the pronoun *she*, there is no danger of accusing the poor job applicants of espionage.]

MISPLACED: We *only* deliver on Tuesdays. [In spoken English we would stress the word *Tuesdays* so that *only* clearly modifies *Tuesdays*. In written English we would usually have to depend on word order to be certain of the meaning, and the word order in our example suggests that *only* modifies *deliver*: We only deliver on Tuesdays rather than ship or receive.

REVISED: We deliver *only* on Tuesdays [*or:* We deliver on Tuesdays *only*.]

Squinting modifiers:
The "squinting" modifier is a special type of misplaced modifier. Its position in the sentence is ambiguous so that it appears to modify either of *two* words. Rewrite so that it refers clearly to one word only.

SQUINTING: The forwarder who was checking the order *hurriedly* answered the phone. [Does *hurriedly* modify *checking* or *answered*?]

REVISED: The forwarder who was checking the order answered the phone *hurriedly*.

mx I MIXED CONSTRUCTION

Revise part of your sentence so that it matches the structure of the other part.

There are two varieties of mixed construction. More commonly, your sentence begins with one grammatical construction, then shifts to another that cannot structurally complete it. Less commonly, you mix figures of speech (comparisons) in some tasteless or inconsistent way that deflects attention from the point you want to make.

STRUCTURAL MISMATCH: *By entering each order as it is completed* is the most efficient way to control the inventory.

The two parts of that sentence do not form a proper fit. The first half (in italics) is an adverb forced to serve as subject of the verb *is*. But only a noun construction or a pronoun can act as a subject. To revise, either provide the sentence with a grammatical subject that is structurally a noun, or let the first part stand as is — an adverb phrase — and write a full main clause after it.

REVISION 1: Entering each order as it is completed is the most efficient way to control the inventory.

Leaving out *By* allows the sentence to begin with the gerund *entering*. A gerund is a verb form ending in *–ing* that acts as a noun. The gerund phrase *Entering each order . . .* is structurally a *noun* and can therefore serve correctly as subject of the sentence.

REVISION 2: By entering each order as it is completed, we can most efficiently control the inventory.

Leaving unchanged the adverbial beginning of the sentence, we turn the second part into a main clause. Now the adverb phrase *By entering . . .* modifies the verb of the main clause, *can . . . control.*

STRUCTURAL MISMATCH: The reason we do not check references is *because* we assume they will be unduly favorable toward the candidate.

Avoid *reason is because* sentences. The linking verb *is* should be followed here by a noun clause or other type of noun that provides *the reason*. Simply change *because* to *that,* and the adverb clause becomes the needed noun clause:

REVISED: The reason we do not check references is *that* we assume they will be unduly favorable toward the candidate.

STRUCTURAL MISMATCH: Just because he is physically handicapped is no reason to suppose the other workers will not accept him.

The error in that sentence is similar to that in the previous example. Now the adverb clause (beginning *Just because*) is awkwardly put into the subject position and made to act as a noun. The easiest correction is to substitute a noun construction for the adverbial *Just because*.

REVISED: *The mere fact that* he is physically handicapped is no reason to suppose the other workers will not accept him.

STRUCTURAL MISMATCH: On the 3rd of June is *when* the letter of credit expires.

Avoid *is when* sentences. A *when* clause is an adverb and should not be put to work — after the verb *is* — as a noun. To correct, omit *is when*.

REVISED: On the 3rd of June the letter of credit expires.

MIXED FIGURES OF SPEECH: Don't let your makeup melt under the cold eye of the sun. [To "melt" under a "cold eye" is a set of clashing images, and the result is either absurd or unintentionally comic — hardly the effect an advertiser wants to produce.]
REVISED: Don't let your makeup melt under the merciless eye of the sun.

MIXED FIGURES: For a white-as-snow wash that's as fresh as a summer breeze, buy Daily detergent.
REVISED: For a clean, white wash that's as fresh as a summer breeze, buy Daisy detergent. [Sometimes one of the figures simply has to be removed.

Rewrite with a positive slant. Do not focus on negative aspects.

Negative expressions leave undesirable impressions on the reader. Try to phrase negative messages in as positive a way as possible. In general, focus on what you *can* do, not on what you cannot do. Avoid blaming or criticizing the reader.

NEGATIVE: You failed to enclose your check in the envelope.
POSITIVE: When your envelope arrived, it contained only your payment stub.

NEGATIVE: We no longer make the item you ordered.
POSITIVE: The item you ordered has been replaced with a new, improved version.

NEGATIVE: We cannot fill your order until after January 12.
POSITIVE: Your order will be filled soon after January 12.

NEGATIVE: Your service contract does not cover you for defects in original design.
POSITIVE: Your service contract specifically covers you for mechanical repairs only

---

num | NUMBERS

Change the indicated numbers to words or the indicated words to numbers.

Here are lists of general and special rules for writing numbers:

GENERAL RULES

1. Numbers that begin sentences. Use words: Fifty-four people were registered.
2. Numbers one through ten. Use words: Four out of five managers agreed.
3. Numbers over ten. Use figures: We found 16 errors in his 20-page report.
4. Mixed numbers (numbers *under* and *over* ten used to refer to the same item or related items). Use figures: Please order 6 files and 24 envelopes.
5. Unrelated numbers placed together. Use a comma as divider: In 1983, 32 workers were promoted.
6. Two number-adjectives placed together. Write the lesser in words: Please use eleven 20-cent stamps and 8 five-cent stamps.
7. Large round numbers. Use figures + words: 3.5 million, 8 billion.

SPECIAL RULES — Addresses

1. House numbers (except *One*). Use figures: 119 Walnut Grove Road, One Park Place.
2. Numerical street names from one to ten. Use words: 330 Fifth Avenue, 210 Eighth Street.
3. Street names over ten. Use ordinal numbers (-st, -nd, -rd, -th): 34 12th Street, 270 42nd Street.
4. State highways, interstates, and routes. Use figures: Route 1, U.S. 66, State Road 7.

Book Divisions, Official Names

5. Number of a page, line, verse, paragraph, figure, note, invoice. Use figures: page 17, line 10, verse 23, paragraph 6, note 2, Purchase Order No. 870.
6. Official names that include numbers. Use words: First Baptist Church, Tenth Ward.

Dates

7. Dates beginning with month. Use figures: March 10, 1984 [*Not* March 10th].
8. Dates followed by month (or month omitted). Use words or ordinals: on the tenth of March, on the 10th of March, on the tenth.
9. Centuries and decades. Use words: the twentieth century, the sixties.

Fractions, decimals, percentages

10. Simple fractions (without whole numbers). Use words: one-sixth minority, three-tenths of a mile.
11. Fractions used with whole numbers. Use figures: 3¼ yards.
12. Percentages. Use figures plus the word *percent:* 10 percent, 0.5 percent.
13. Decimals. Use figures: 0.4 inch, a .22 caliber rifle.

Measurements

14. Quantities, measurements, degrees, sizes. Use figures: 1 quart, 6 pounds, over 12,000 votes, 98.6° F, size 9½.
15. Very large quantities. Use figure + word: We sold 8 million copies last year.

Money

16. Exact and approximate money amounts. Use figures: a pen for $2.50, a $40 blouse, nearly $1,000. [Do not use a period and zeroes — a $40.00 blouse — for a whole-dollar amount.]
17. Cents alone. Use figures plus the word *cents:* 5 cents, 80 cents' worth.

18. Money used as adjective. Use words: a five-dollar book, a three-hundred-dollar suit.

19. Money in legal documents. (Do not use this style in other business writing.) Use words followed by figures in parentheses: three hundred dollars ($300).

20. Mixed money amounts. Be consistent: a $3.25 book and a $.49 pen, a ten-dollar book and a fifty-cent pen.

Time, Age, Anniversaries

21. Time with a.m., p.m., noon, and midnight. Use figures: 11:30 a.m., 8 p.m., [not 8:00 p.m.], 12 noon, between 11:30 p.m. and 1 a.m.

22. Time with *o'clock*. Use either words or figures. Words are considered the more formal choice. FORMAL: ten o'clock. INFORMAL: 10 o'clock. [But do not use *o'clock* with *a.m.* or *p.m.*]

23. Exact ages. Use words: a ten-year-old boy, five months old, age fifty-eight.

EXCEPTION: For exact ages, use *numbers* in statistical material, in formal documents, and when age is stated precisely in years, months, and days: 3 years, 6 months, and 13 days old.

24. Approximate ages. Use words: about forty, in her thirties.

25. Anniversaries expressed in over two words. Use ordinals: 150th anniversary.

26. Anniversaries expressed in one or two words. Use words: his twenty-first birthday, their fifth anniversary.

---

open | OPENING

Open your communication with an approach designed to build good will.

Good will is a vital objective in all business communication. Every letter or report should strive to improve the reader's regard for your organization. The reward, of course, will be higher profits and better public relations. Even if you must offer unpleasant news, try to make your reader understand your position. A business can never afford to lose a customer.

TYPES OF OPENING

Three basic openings are used in business writing to produce the best possible reaction in the reader, no matter what the reason for the communication. In general, imagine yourself in the reader's place. If *you* were the worried customer, how would *you* like to be informed of good news — or of bad news?

If *you* were the anxious job seeker, how could *you* begin your letter so as to engage the attention of a personnel director swamped with applications? The three openings used to communicate most effectively with your reader are

1. the *positive*
2. the *buffered*
3. the *persuasive*.

1. Positive opening. Put the best news first.

The positive opening is used for communications that inform readers of something they will be happy to hear or at least something they will receive neutrally. For example, an order is being filled, credit has been granted, or a full refund is on its way. The positive opening simply means that the best news is put first. Do not open with a "thank you for your order" when the best news from the reader's standpoint is not your courtesy, but the fact that the order will be shipped next Tuesday. Put yourself in your reader's shoes, decide which information will receive the warmest welcome, and open with it. (See also YOU-VIEWPOINT, TACT, and READER ADVANTAGE.)

2. Buffered opening. Cushion bad news with a "buffer" — a positive opening.

Use a buffered opening whenever you must inform readers of something they would not like to hear. Avoid starting out with bad news. Try a sensitive opening that not only cushions the blow but also points out whatever might be positive in the situation. Few messages are so negative that no buffer can be found to open with. But if nothing truly positive occurs to you, your last resort might be to thank the reader sincerely for informing you of the problem.

Price increases, order delays, a rejected job application — all would be conveyed best through buffers. The buffered approach not only *opens* with something positive but also *closes* on an affirmative note as well. The middle paragraphs explain why *no* is the answer, but the end expresses at least the hope that at some other time or in some other capacity your organization might serve the reader. No business can afford angry or disgruntled customers.

BAD NEWS: We cannot repair your car free of charge because your warranty has expired.
BUFFER: Thank you for writing us about the problem you are having with your car's radiator.

BAD NEWS: We regret to inform you that we hired someone with more experience for the sales-manager opening.
BUFFER: Your excellent qualifications for our sales-manager opening were carefully considered before we reached a decision.

BAD NEWS: This agency will not reimburse you for duty taxes you paid on your camera because these taxes are the purchaser's responsibility.

BUFFER: Mr. Smith, I hope you had a restful vacation despite the duty taxes you had to pay on your camera.

3. Persuasive opening. Hook the reader from the start.

Use the persuasive opening for sales letters or any business communication that aims to bring the reader around to the writer's point of view. Even job application letters would use the persuasive opening. This opening employs a tactic that engages the reader's attention immediately. Routine openings defeat this goal. Instead, find some great selling point about your side of the situation and place it first to catch the reader's eye.

BLAH: I saw your ad for an entry-level accountant in the *Bulletin* yesterday.

PERSUASIVE: Could Jonson Manufacturing use an industrious, experienced, and accurate accountant?

BLAH: Solar water-heating systems are economical.

PERSUASIVE: You can reduce your fuel bills by 80 percent with a Sunnyside solar water-heating system.

¶ | PARAGRAPH

Start a new paragraph at the place indicated.

FORMAT

In business communication several styles exist for signalling the beginning of a paragraph. The most traditional format involves skipping a line at the end of the previous paragraph and then *indenting* (starting several spaces to the right of the margin) the first line of the new paragraph. Also widely used is "block" style, in which you skip a line but do not indent. Other methods include indenting all lines *but* the first, using dashes or a series of periods, or numbering each paragraph. Whatever style you choose, use it consistently throughout any piece of business writing.

THE PARAGRAPH AS A SUBUNIT

The beginning of each new paragraph marks a new stage in the development of your total communication. Just as sentences are the largest subunits of a paragraph, so paragraphs are the largest subunits of your letter or report. A paragraph does not begin and end just anywhere. The main idea of your communication needs to be developed in each of its important *aspects,* and a new paragraph signals the shift to a new aspect of the whole message. For example, if you were writing a short report summarizing sales activities in five selected regions of the country, it is likely that you would write an introductory paragraph briefly mentioning your purpose, including the five regions you will treat. Then you will probably devote one paragraph to each sales region. Your report would naturally break down, therefore, into at least six paragraphs that form natural subdivisions of the whole.

STRUCTURE OF A PARAGRAPH

Many writers were taught in high school never to write a one-sentence paragraph. Yet in business communications one-sentence paragraphs at the beginning and end of a piece of writing are both common and acceptable. Sales writers often use one-sentence openers to enhance the attention-getting effect that an introductory statement should have. For improved readability business communications in general use shorter paragraphs than are found in many other kinds of writing. The more complex your communication, the more important it is to use short, frequent paragraphs linked with transitional words, phrases, or statements to aid the reader's memory and comprehension.

The middle paragraphs of business correspondence normally consist of at least two sentences. One sentence, usually the first, is the *topic sentence,* which states the general idea (topic) of the paragraph. The following sentence or sentences should keep to the topic (see IRRELEVANT and UNITY) and develop it through the use of facts, figures, details, examples, explanations, definitions, arguments, or any other logical technique of organization, including a combination of such techniques.

There are three main organizational features to a well-structured paragraph:

1. *unity,* the relevance of all sentences to the topic sentence and the avoidance of digressions.

2. *development,* elaboration of the main idea with enough details, examples, and arguments to give the impression of full or adequate treatment.

3. *coherence,* the connection between one sentence and the next in a logical pattern.

The use of *transitions* is an essential means of achieving coherence. Transitions are expressions that show the logical relationships between ideas. Transitions are accomplished in four main ways:

a. through the use of certain standard transitional words or phrases (*for example, however, in fact, thus, therefore, in conclusion, to be sure*)

b. through repetition of key words or ideas

c. through pronouns

d. through demonstrative adjectives (*this, that, these, those*).

(For more information on paragraph structure, see COHERENCE, IRRELEVANT, TRANSITION, and UNITY.)

The following paragraph illustrates unity, development, and coherence. Transitions are in parentheses, and the topic sentence is printed in italics. The abbreviations stand for *transitional phrase* or *word, repetition, demonstrative adjective,* and *pronoun.*

SAMPLE PARAGRAPH: *After reviewing the two proposals, I recommend that we adopt*

the steam system from Commercial Plumbing rather than the individual unit heaters

                Trans. Phrase   Rep.

from Heat-Tech. (To be sure,) (the individual heaters) require less expense to install,

  Rep.   Rep.   Dem. Adj.

take up (less) space, and need (less) maintenance. (These) considerations are,

Trans. Phrase   Trans. Word   Rep.

(of course,) important ones. (Nevertheless,) the (Commercial system) will save money

                        Pron.   Rep.   Pron. + Rep.

in the long run. Over a ten-year period, (it) will consume (less) fuel and (it) (will) be

more easily upgraded for increased heat output.

---

paral [//] | PARALLELISM

Make sentence parts similar (parallel) in form if they are similar in function.

In sentence structure *parallelism* is the technique of expressing units of meaning that perform related functions by means of word groups that are similar in structure. If your purpose, for example, is to mention briefly your reasons for choosing a certain supplier, the skeleton structure of your sentence is likely to resemble this: I chose supplier X because (1), because (2), and because (3). The numbers 1, 2, and 3 stand for three reasons; and since they are similar in function (each of the three provides a *reason*), they should be cast in three parallel word groups, each beginning with *because.*

LACK OF PARALLELISM: These crackers are crisp, buttery, and *go well with all kinds of foods.*
PARALLEL: These crackers are crisp, buttery, and versatile. [Three closely related ideas are now expressed in parallel form by three adjectives instead of two adjectives and a verb.]

LACK OF PARALLELISM: Jeff mixes our custom paints with dexterity, patience, and *takes pride in it.*
PARALLEL: Jeff mixes our custom paints with dexterity, patience, and pride.

LACK OF PARALLELISM: To do well in business, one should have good interpersonal skills, demonstrating excellent communication skills is important, and so is being hardworking.

PARALLEL: To do well in business, one should have good interpersonal skills, demonstrate excellent communication skills, and be hardworking. [After *one should* we now have three parallel word groups, each beginning with a verb: *have, demonstrate,* and *be.*]

Lack of parallelism can at times distort meaning.

LACK OF PARALLELISM: The export declaration attests that the goods are of a specific value and we are not selling them illegally.

PARALLEL: The export declaration attests that the goods are of a specific value and *that* we are not selling them illegally. [The first sentence seems to end with an undocumented statement by the writer. The second version makes it clear that the export declaration, and not the mere word of the writer, is attesting to the legality of the matter.]

---

paren ( ) | PARENTHESES

Use parentheses around material that can be considered extra information, material that is not essential to the meaning of your sentence.

Using parentheses in writing is like whispering extra information to your readers, information that, in a pinch, you could afford to leave out. Parentheses are rare in business writing because one of the goals of business communication is to be concise — to leave out unnecessary details and get to the point. Parentheses tend to de-emphasize information. If you do *not* wish to de-emphasize the material inside your parentheses, then try setting it off with commas instead. In general, do not use parentheses where commas would do.

In business writing there are several appropriate uses for parentheses:

1. For unimportant but helpful details:

- Bulletin 83CDX (an updated version of 82CDX) describes briefly each product in our line.

- Style No. 153 (the one with the highest price) includes a maintenance kit.

2. For reference notations:

* The Chart F-1 (see pp. 12-14) lists the pertinent qualities of the new accounts-payable software program.

3. For money amounts: In legal documents, money amounts are often written twice, once in words and then as numbers within parentheses, to eliminate the possibility of misreading. Do not imitate this style in other business writing:

* Lessee agrees to pay a rental fee of three hundred fifty dollars ($350) on the first of each month.

4. Numbers and letters marking items in a list:

* Please have available (1) an overhead projector, (2) a blackboard, and (3) a 16mm movie projector at the seminar location. [No *periods* are used after numbers or letters enclosed in parentheses.]

If, however, the listed items are arranged vertically and are separate from the paragraph, use numbers *without* parentheses, and place a period after each number.

* At the seminar location, please have available

    1. an overhead projector

    2. a blackboard

    3. a 16 mm movie projector

MISUSE OF PARENTHESES:

ERROR: Model 153 (not 135) is the one without a negative charge lead wire.
REVISED: Model 153, not 135, is the one without a negative charge lead wire.

NOTE: Do not use parentheses where commas would be preferable. Remember that parentheses tend to de-emphasize. In this example, however, the *importance* of the distinction between the two model numbers indicates that commas are necessary to set off the phrase.

ERROR: His (Rick's) supervisor told her (Alice) to use a torque wrench.
REVISED: Rick's supervisor told Alice to use a torque wrench.

NOTE: Do not solve your pronoun-reference problems by inserting proper names in parentheses. Avoid such unnecessary awkwardness by recasting the sentence and using proper names *instead* of pronouns.

> In general, avoid the passive voice of verbs in business writing (This page *was typed by me*) and prefer the active voice (I *typed this page*). The passive voice tends to be indirect, impersonal, and wordy compared to the active voice.

When you use a verb in the *active* voice, the doer of the verb's actions is also the grammatical subject.

• Ellen answered the phone an hour ago. [*Ellen* is both doer and grammatical subject of the verb answered.]

When you use a verb in the *passive* voice, the doer of the verb's action is either (1) de-emphasized and delayed so that it winds up as the object of a preposition or (2) drops out of sight altogether.

1. The phone was answered by Ellen an hour ago.
2. The phone was answered an hour ago.

Notice how the change from the indirect and even evasive passive voice to the direct active voice improves the following sentences:

PASSIVE: A meeting was held in the main dining hall by all the committee members.
ACTIVE: All the committee members held a meeting in the main dining hall. [Fewer words, more directness.]

PASSIVE: All the blueprints were run with just enough fluid for a clear copy. [Who ran them?]
ACTIVE: Lisa ran all the blueprints with just enough fluid for a clear copy.

PASSIVE: It will be seen from the invoice that our terms allow a 2 percent discount for cash payments.
ACTIVE: You will see from the invoice that our terms allow a 2 percent discount for cash payments. [*You* is more personal than *it*.]

PROPER USE OF PASSIVE VOICE

Sometimes the passive voice is the right choice. Obviously, if you do not *know* the doer of the verb's action, the passive voice is all you can use: The original was left in the photocopier.

The passive voice may also be the right choice if you do not want to sound as if you are accusing somebody of something.

- The accounting summary was accidentally erased from the memory banks. [This sounds much less critical than "John accidentally erased the accounting summary from the memory banks."]

Finally, when you want to stress the receiver of the action rather than the doer of the action, the passive voice is appropriate.

- The president of the company will be interviewed on the evening news tonight. [In this case, the company president is of more interest than the interviewer.]

pro | PRONOUN REFERENCE

Make the marked pronoun refer unmistakably to a single previous word, a noun or another pronoun, called the antecedent.

The *antecedent* is the word that a pronoun refers to. For example, in the sentence *The boss lost his temper,* the antecedent of the pronoun *his* is the noun *boss.* Problems in pronoun reference fall into two categories.

1. DANGLING PRONOUNS

Dangling pronouns have no antecedent. They are often used to refer to a whole idea that has not been cast in the form of a single *noun,* but rather in the form of a *main clause* — even a whole previous sentence. Watch out for the pronouns *which, this,* and *it,* for they are the ones most often found dangling.

UNCLEAR REFERENCE: The best way to learn to use the stencil duplicator is to follow the operations manual step by step, *which* will prevent a costly mistake. [The dangling *which* needs an antecedent. It is forced to refer ungrammatically to the whole preceding main clause.]

REVISION 1: The best way to learn to use the stencil duplicator is to follow the operations manual step by step, *a method* which will prevent a costly mistake. [Insert a noun before *which* that logically sums up the whole idea of the main clause before it.]

REVISION 2: The best way to learn to use the stencil duplicator is to follow the operations manual step by step *and thereby* prevent a costly mistake. [Simply rework the sentence to eliminate the troublesome *which* clause.]

UNCLEAR REFERENCE: Tom Keenan is our company advertising director. He designs all of our graphics, and he also heads our monthly sales meetings. *This* keeps him very busy. [The pronoun *this* refers loosely to the ideas in two previous main clauses. Use revision techniques that apply to *which.*]

REVISION 1: Tom Keenan is our company advertising director. He designs all our graphics, and he also heads our monthly sales meetings. *These responsibilities* keep him very busy.

REVISION 2: Tom Keenan is our company advertising director. He designs all our graphics, and he also heads our monthly sales meetings, *responsibilities that* keep him very busy.

UNCLEAR REFERENCE: *They* said on the news that there will be an increase in the gasoline tax. [Who are *they?* Avoid statements that begin *They said* or *It said.*]
REVISED: *I heard* on the news that there will be an increase in the gasoline tax.

UNCLEAR REFERENCE: When Mr. Raffa misses an appointment, *it* is always blamed on his secretary. [The pronoun *it* is used improperly to refer to the *when* clause, an adverb.]
REVISED: When Mr. Raffa misses an appointment, *he* always blames *his mistake* on his secretary. [First, change from passive voice — *it is . . . blamed* — to active voice — *he . . . blames.* Next, use a noun that logically sums up the idea in the *when* clause — *his mistake* in place of *it.*]

2. AMBIGUOUS PRONOUNS

Sometimes it is unclear which of two previous nouns a pronoun refers to. This situation opens a statement to double meaning or ambiguity.

AMBIGUOUS: When Linda talked to Gail yesterday, *she* said the layouts should be ready Tuesday. [Which *she* set the layout deadline, Linda or Gail?]
REVISED: Gail told Linda yesterday that the layouts should be ready Tuesday.

AMBIGUOUS: Although all copiers can provide reproductions, *they* vary greatly in quality. [Which varies greatly in quality — the copies or the copiers?]
REVISED: Although they all can provide reproductions, copiers vary greatly in quality.

---

quot "/" | QUOTATION MARKS

Use quotation marks to set off (1) directly quoted words, (2) words given special emphasis, (3) words referred to *as* words, and (4) the titles of *parts* of a book, magazine, or newspaper.

1. QUOTATION MARKS TO SET OFF THE DIRECTLY QUOTED WORDS OF A WRITER OR SPEAKER:

• The bonded messenger said, "There is little chance of getting this letter delivered by four o'clock."

- "There is little chance," said the bonded messenger, "of getting this letter delivered by four o'clock." [When the words identifying the speaker — *said the bonded messenger* — break up the quoted sentence, they are set off with commas. Each *part* of the interrupted quotation is then enclosed in quotation marks.]

Do not use quotation marks to set off an indirect quotation.

- The bonded messenger said that there was little chance of getting this letter delivered by four o'clock. [Indirect quotation reports what someone said *at one remove*. The word *that* often introduces an indirect quotation.]

Do not use quotation marks for long quotations. When quoting over three typewritten lines, *indent* both sides of the passage and use single-spacing.

- The author sums up the emotional impact of the term *pollution* with these words:

> Now that pollution has become a pressing problem of the sixties and seventies, it has become a household word. As with most sociological issues, it is difficult to separate fact from emotion. Pollution thus becomes a subject for the political arena, further charging the emotional aspect and clouding the facts.
>
> — R. D. Ross
> *Air Pollution and Industry*

2. QUOTATION MARKS TO SET OFF WORDS GIVEN SPECIAL EMPHASIS.

Technical jargon and slang (terms to be distinguished from the writer's normal vocabulary) and expressions following words like *marked, stamped,* or *signed,* should be quoted.

- In the printing trade, a "font" is a collection of type of the same style and size. ["Font" is a technical term.]
- According to his co-workers, Hanley is a "real neat guy" in all but the way he dresses. [Slang.]
- Stamp the order "Rush" if you want to expedite service.

3. QUOTATION MARKS TO SET OFF WORDS USED *AS* WORDS.

Words to be defined and words referred to *as* words are set off by quotation marks in *informal* settings. In *formal* settings such words are underlined or italicized.

- The accounting term "disbursement" means paying out.
- I think your letter uses the word "and" too often.

4. QUOTATION MARKS TO SET OFF THE TITLES OF *PARTS* OF BOOKS, NEWSPAPERS, OR MAGAZINES AND THE TITLES OF TV AND RADIO PROGRAMS AND OF UNPUBLISHED MANUSCRIPTS.

The titles of books, magazines, and newspapers should be underlined (italicized), but the parts of those publications — chapters, articles, short stories, short poems, sermons, and songs — are enclosed by quotation marks.

Do not quote or underline the title at the head of your *own* report. Simply set it off by starting the report a few lines below it.

- Chapter: "Data Processing — Developing Listening Skills" in *Let's Talk Business.*
- Article: "Holland in Bloom" in the *Providence Sunday Journal.*
- Lecture: Professor Bottorgg's "New Performance Standards in the Automotive Industry."
- Television program: "60 Minutes."

USING QUOTATION MARKS WITH OTHER PUNCTUATION

a. Place periods and commas *inside* closing quotation marks.

- The guidelines they gave us were called "evaluation criteria."
- "The sales department takes care of all catalog updates," she said.

b. Place colons and semicolons *outside* closing quotation marks.

- We found that several pieces of equipment had been "borrowed"; namely, three typewriters, a video tape recorder, and a photocopier.

c. Place question marks, exclamation points, dashes, and parentheses *inside* closing quotation marks *if they are part of the quotation.*

- He asked, "Where is the heavy-duty stapler?"
- Wesley exclaimed, "The wiring is smoking!"

d. Place question marks, exclamation points, dashes, and parentheses *outside* closing quotation marks *if they are not part of the quotation.*

- Did she say, "I haven't seen the general ledger yet"?
- "Capital, organization, and contacts" — this last necessity is the one we lack — "are all that is required to start a business," he assured us.

e. Do not use more than one end mark with closing marks.

ERROR: She said, "When will the Harris presentation be ready?". [Omit the period.]

f. Use single quotation marks to set off a quotation *within* a quotation ("'/'").

- The placement assistant said, "My superior told me, 'Never give references over the telephone.'"

g. Use brackets [ ] for editorial insertions within quotations. See BRACKETS.

Show readers the advantages to them of thinking or acting as you want them to.

Try to do two things in every business communication: (1) get your basic message across and (2) build goodwill — positive feelings in your readers toward your organization. Never miss a chance to point out the advantages your readers will enjoy from ordering your products or using your services. Do not stress what *you* want from your readers but rather what you can offer *them*. (See also TACT and YOU-VIEWPOINT.)

COMPANY ADVANTAGE: We have over 40 different styles and sizes of Roadwear tires to choose from.
READER ADVANTAGE: You will certainly find a Roadwear tire to fit your car and your budget because we make them in 40 different styles and sizes.

COMPANY ADVANTAGE: You are invited to help us celebrate a great year in sales at our annual trade show.
READER ADVANTAGE: Please come to our annual trade show and help us celebrate *you,* our finest patrons, with special prices on this year's line before it is advertised for the general public.

COMPANY ADVANTAGE: Please send us your check for $73.92 for your overdue bill.
READER ADVANTAGE: To maintain your excellent credit rating, please send $73.92 for your overdue bill.

NOTE: You may have to spend *extra* words in demonstrating to a reader the advantages of following your suggestions, but they are never *wasted* words.

___

rep | REPETITION

Do not repeat words, phrases, or ideas needlessly.

Repetitious phrasing tends to be unimaginative and stylistically dull. The repetition of ideas — whether in the same or somewhat different words — is the more serious problem because the writer appears to have little to say and readers feel that their time is being wasted. Repetition for *emphasis,* however, can sometimes be effective. (See also PARAGRAPH and WORDINESS.)

REPETITIOUS PHRASING: I am very interested in obtaining copies of your *interesting* bulletin "Creative Gardening."

REVISED: I am very interested in obtaining copies of your informative bulletin "Creative Gardening." [Vary your word choice.]

I am very interested in obtaining copies of your bulletin "Creative Gardening." [Simply omit unnecessary words.]

REPETITIOUS PHRASING: You will be glad to hear that you can obtain flight insurance at most airports. You simply purchase the insurance from a machine or from an on-site insurance agent. You can be insured for up to $100,000 during the flight. [Overuse of *insurance* and *flight*.]

REVISED: You will be glad to hear that you can obtain flight insurance at most airports by purchasing it from a machine or an on-site insurance agent. You can get coverage of up to $100,000.

REPETITION OF IDEAS: The 200-mile fishing limit has increased the profits of most professional fishing companies and has extended the fishing area to 200 miles.

REVISED: The 200-mile fishing limit has increased the profits of most professional fishing companies.

Redundancies: Certain expressions are redundant; they say the same thing twice. Avoid such redundancies as

- cooperate *together*
- raise *up*
- repeat that *again*
- continue *on*

Deliberate repetition: Repetition for emphasis is on occasion desirable in effective writing.

- The motivation of employees in the early 1900s was survival; the motivation of employees by the 1960s was self-satisfaction. [Use of repetition to highlight a contrast.]
- He was indifferent — indifferent to public opinion and indifferent to profit motive. [Repetition to stress the main point.]

RO | RUN-ON SENTENCE

Do not connect two sentences without proper punctuation.

The run-on sentence simply leaves out punctuation between two sentences. This error is similar to a comma splice, in which two sentences are connected

by incorrect punctuation — a comma. (See COMMA SPLICE.)
Run-on sentences can be corrected in several ways:

RUN-ON: The secretary stored 25 annual reports as file copies then she shredded the remainder.

REVISION 1: The secretary stored 25 annual reports as file copies. Then she shredded the remainder. [Use a period.]

REVISION 2: The secretary stored 25 annual reports as file copies; then she shredded the remainder. [Use a semicolon if the two sentences are closely related. See SEMI-COLON.]

REVISION 3: The secretary stored 25 annual reports as file copies, and then she shredded the remainder. [Use a comma and a coordinating conjunction such as *and, but, or, nor, for, yet.*]

semi [;] I SEMICOLON

Use a semicolon between elements of equal grammatical structure.

A semicolon is used in the following two types of structures:

Main clause; main clause

Sentence element containing a comma; sentence element containing a comma

1. SEMICOLON BETWEEN MAIN CLAUSES

When two complete sentences (main clauses) are closely related in both form and content, a semicolon will emphasize their special relationship.

* We do not manufacture thermometers; we are specialists in thermostat devices.

With conjunctive adverbs: Semicolons should be used before *conjunctive adverbs,* adverbs acting as transitions between two main clauses. Some of the most common conjunctive adverbs are *besides, consequently, furthermore, hence, however, indeed, instead, likewise, moreover, nevertheless, otherwise, then, therefore, thus.*

* You can lease a Drive-Away at any time you like; *however,* a security deposit is requested when you make reservations.

With transitional phrases: Semicolons should be used before *transitional phrases* that link two main clauses. Some of the most common transitional phrases are *after all, at any rate, for example, in addition, in fact, in other words, on the contrary, on the other hand.*

* Public response to our new product line has been great; *for example,* 1,400 Model 3B's have been sold in California alone.

NOTE: Two transitions — *namely* and *for example* — sometimes do not introduce a main clause, but use a semicolon before them anyway.

* The stockroom is low on several catalogs; *namely, the full-line catalog, the paint strainer catalog, and the paint sprayer catalog.* [The italicized portion of the sentence is *not* a main clause.]

2. SEMICOLON BETWEEN SENTENCE ELEMENTS ALREADY CONTAINING COMMAS

Use the semicolon to show the clear divisions between a parallel series of sentence elements when each element itself contains a comma.

* We toured factories in Fredricksburg, Virginia; Piedmont, Ohio; Clarksville, Indiana; and Des Moines, Iowa.
* We toured factories of our choice on June 12, 1983; July 15, 1983; and August 13, 1983.

NOTE: Generally, do not use a semicolon if you connect two main clauses with a coordinating conjunction such as *and, but, for.* However, according to Rule 2, a semicolon is needed between two main clauses *if at least one comma is used within either of the main clauses.*

* Tuesday, July 18, is the layout deadline; *but* you have a week longer, possibly two, to submit the cover graphics.

sexist | SEXIST EXPRESSIONS

Avoid terms that refer to only one sex when both sexes are intended.

Your choice of pronouns and occupational titles should reflect equal treatment of the sexes whenever possible. Especially avoid labeling an occupation as belonging particularly to one sex. If you use the word *foreman,* for instance, you may suggest to your readers — even without meaning to — that you assume anyone in charge of a work crew to be a male. Although such language is in common use, it is nevertheless considered sexist, implying prejudice against one of the sexes. Instead of *foreman* you might use a sexually neutral term like *supervisor* or *section head.* A group of common sexist expressions and their nondiscriminatory alternatives follows:

SEXIST	ALTERNATIVE
businessman	business executive, business owner, business person, company head, manufacturer, wholesaler
congressman	representative
fireman	firefighter
foreman	supervisor
housewife	housekeeper
manpower	workers, work force
repairman	service technician
salesman	sales representative, salesperson
workman	worker, laborer, employee

Your choice of pronouns, too, can be regarded as sexist. Avoid the real sexism of occupational stereotyping. Do not automatically refer to a secretary as *she* or a member of the board as *he*. Also, avoid the apparent sexism inherent in the language itself. In English there is no singular personal pronoun that refers to either a man or a woman. The male pronouns *he, him,* or *his* have traditionally referred to both men and women in situations where the sex of the antecedent is not identified. A sentence like the following used to be perfectly acceptable: Everyone has *his* own time card. Now, however, the tendency is to avoid such pronoun usage, and there are several simple ways to overcome reliance upon a masculine pronoun:

1. Make the antecedent plural.

SEXIST: A manager should strive to bring out the best in every employee *he* supervises.
NEUTRAL: *Managers* should strive to bring out the best in every employee *they* supervise.

2. Rewrite to eliminate need for a pronoun.

• A manager should strive to bring out the best in every employee.

3. Use a double pronoun.

• A manager should strive to bring out the best in every employee *he* or *she* supervises. [This solution — *he* or *she, her* or *him, his* or *her* — is awkward and should be used sparingly.]

Finally, terms such as *doctor, lawyer, teacher,* or *police officer* refer to both men and women. Do not use unnecessary adjectives — woman doctor, female police officer — unless it is important to indicate sex.

• City Hospital employs only five women doctors.

• She was the first female police officer in the county to be promoted to the rank of detective.

> Do not shift needlessly or illogically
> between different pronoun or verb forms:
> 1. Pronouns should agree in *number* and
>   *person.*
> 2. Verbs should agree in *tense, voice,* and
>   *mood.*

The pronouns and verbs in your sentences determine your "point of view." Make sure that your point of view is consistent within the individual sentence, from sentence to sentence, and from paragraph to paragraph until a shift is justified by a change in the nature of what you are writing.

1. PRONOUN SHIFTS

Avoid shifts in *number.* You produce a shift in pronoun number when you change from a singular to a plural pronoun, or vice versa, while still referring to the same noun.

SHIFT: Microchips are becoming more compact and powerful each year while, incredible as it may seem, *its* cost keeps going down.
REVISED: Microchips are becoming more compact and powerful each year while, incredible as it may seem, *their* cost keeps going down.

Many shifts in number involve the singular pronouns *anybody, anyone, everybody, everyone, somebody, someone, each, either, neither,* and *no one.* These pronouns often cause special problems.

SHIFT: Each committee member contributed *their* time and energy to writing the proposal.
REVISED: Each committee member contributed *his* or *her* time and energy to writing the proposal. [This is an acceptable but awkward solution. See SEXIST EXPRESSIONS.]
BETTER: *All committee members* contributed *their* time and energy to writing the proposal.

Avoid shifts in *person.* Personal pronouns occur in three persons:

1. First-person pronouns include *I, me, my, we, our.*
2. Second-person pronouns include *you, your, yours.*
3. Third-person pronouns include *he, him, she, her, it, one, they, them, their.*

If it is not logically necessary, do not shift pronoun persons.

SHIFT: *Everyone* should prepare a professional résumé, and *you* should update it whenever *you* change jobs.
REVISED: *You* should prepare a professional résumé, and *you* should update it whenever you change jobs.

SHIFT: If *one* tries hard enough, *you* can master any task.
REVISED: If one tries hard enough, *one* can master any task.

2. VERB SHIFTS

Avoid shifts in *tense*. Tense is the *time* of a verb's action (past, present, or future: see TENSE). Unnecessary shifts in tense — within the same sentence, between sentences, or from paragraph to paragraph — work against clear communication.

SHIFT: The new form *meets* most of the requirements of our inventory system, yet it *had* no place to record back orders.
REVISED: The new form *meets* most of the requirements of our inventory system, yet it *has* no place to record back orders.

SHIFT: The architect *noted* the changes, and then the engineer *designs* them.
REVISED: The architect *noted* the changes, and then the engineer *designed* them.

Avoid shifts in *voice*. Do not change needlessly from the active to the passive voice (see PASSIVE VOICE).

SHIFT: You will hear an error beep if an invalid code *is entered* on the computer. [When you use the active voice, the *logical* subject of a verb is also kept as its *grammatical* subject. In this sentence the verb *enter* — whose logical and grammatical subject is *you* — has been unnecessarily shifted into the passive voice — *is entered*.]
REVISED: You will hear an error beep if *you enter* an invalid code on the computer.

Avoid shifts in *mood*. A verb in English can be in one of three moods — indicative, imperative, or subjunctive. The indicative mood is by far the most common. Sentences that are statements or questions use verbs in the indicative mood.

* Every day our nation wastes products that are vital to tomorrow.
* Do you know what a codicil is?

We use the imperative mood to give commands, often with the pronoun *you* understood or implied as the subject: Turn the dial clockwise. A frequent shift in mood is from imperative to indicative.

SHIFT: *Collect* all the data you can, and then *you must* submit a report.
REVISED: *Collect* all the data you can, and then *submit* a report. [Now both verbs are in the imperative.]

The subjunctive mood occurs rarely in English and only with regard to unlikely future events or mere possibilities, not facts. The most common error involving the subjunctive is the use of the indicative *was* instead of the subjunctive *were* in *if* clauses expressing a condition clearly contrary to fact.

ERROR: If I *was* a better typist, I would have finished by now.
CORRECTED: If I *were* a better typist, I would have finished by now.

For *if* clauses that are *not* clearly contrary to fact, use the indicative.

CORRECT: It looks as if someone was trying to break into the office. [Someone may indeed have been trying to break in.]

sinc I SINCERITY

Show personal interest in your reader through a tone of genuine warmth and a readiness to serve.

An attitude of genuine concern for clients and customers pays off immediately in goodwill for your company. A tone of sincerity in your communications is one of the best means to serve the interests of your organization. Follow these suggestions to communicate your sincerity:

1. Put yourself in your readers' place. How would you like to be treated if you were in their shoes?

2. Do more than the reader asks. Offer suggestions, grant a discount, enclose a coupon, volunteer some useful information. (See CONVERSATIONAL, COURTESY, READER ADVANTAGE.)

3. Avoid trite expressions. These meaningless phrases sound insincere. (See TRITENESS.)

4. Use a warm, conversational style. Avoid sounding impersonal. Write like a human being, not a machine. Pretend you are talking face to face with the reader — but leave out the slang, contractions, and overly casual phrasing of conversation.

5. Avoid jargon, pretentious vocabulary, and any other terms that might annoy or intimidate a reader.

6. Do not "lay it on too thick." Overpraising your product, service, or reader in the attempt to sound sincere will most probably backfire.

Some of these suggestions are illustrated in the following examples:

INSINCERE (TRITE): Please do not hesitate to contact us should you have any questions.
BETTER: Just call me if you have any questions.

INSINCERE (PRETENTIOUS JARGON): Remuneration for consultation will be ascribed to the appropriate account on a per diem basis.
BETTER: You will be billed by the day when you use our consulting service.

INSINCERE (IMPERSONAL): I regret to inform you that a clerical error was made on your last statement. Your corrected statement is enclosed. Please accept our apologies.
BETTER: Is my face red! I made a mistake in calculating your last statement. A corrected statement is enclosed along with my apology.

INSINCERE ("LAID ON THICK"): These beautiful, elegant, genuine-leather-bound, limited-edition classics will be the perfect addition to your library. But hurry! At these incredibly low, low prices, they will go fast.
BETTER: These elegant, leather-bound classics can be added to your library at reasonable cost.

INSINCERE (IMPERSONAL): Enclosed are our latest price catalogs.
BETTER: Here is a set of our latest price catalogs. I circled any price changes on your standard order items so you can easily find them.

split | SPLIT INFINITIVE

Avoid splitting infinitives unnecessarily.

An infinitive consists of the word *to* plus a verb (*to speak, to type*). You split an infinitive by placing a word between the *to* and the verb. In business writing split infinitives are acceptable if they read smoothly and cannot be avoided, but they often result in awkward phrasing. Do not split an infinitive unless doing so is *the only way* to be clear and sound natural.

AWKWARD SPLIT: You must fill out a Travel and Expense Report *to,* according to the Accounting Department, *receive* reimbursement for your trip.
REVISED: According to the Accounting Department, you must fill out a Travel and Expense Report *to receive* reimbursement for your trip.

UNNECESSARY SPLIT: For every $10,000 we spend on resource allocation, we manage *to* usually *cut* our expenses by $35,000.
REVISED: For every $10,000 we spend on resource allocation, we usually manage *to cut* our expenses by $35,000.

ACCEPTABLE SPLIT: We will make every effort *to* politely *advise* the vice president of MacGregor and Kohl that the shipment error was theirs. [If you place *politely* anywhere else — such as after *effort* or *Kohl* — the sentence will lose smoothness.]

ACCEPTABLE SPLIT: We did not want *to* prematurely *suggest* switching to our higher-powered model, but we now think that to be your best solution. [If *prematurely* is placed anywhere else, it would seem to modify the wrong verb.]

SS | SENTENCE STRUCTURE

Rewrite your sentence to improve its clarity, logic, or grammar.

A sentence marked *SS* may involve one or more of the many specific sentence-structure errors dealt with in this manual (CHOPPY SENTENCES, COHERENCE, DANGLING MODIFIER, FRAGMENT, MIXED CONSTRUCTION, PARALLELISM, or RUN-ON SENTENCE). A sentence-structure error often occurs through your *inattention* to the grammatical pattern you begin with — so that you unwittingly switch to a different pattern in midstream.

Usually, if you read the sentence aloud, you will *hear* the problem. If you cannot detect it by ear, simply rewrite the sentence completely, using a different structural pattern (see VARIETY IN SENTENCE PATTERNS and SUBORDINATION).

sub | SUBORDINATION

Cast your more important ideas in the form of main clauses and your less important ideas in lesser grammatical constructions such as subordinate clauses, phrases, or single words.

SUBORDINATION

In sentence structure, subordination is a technique by which you make clear the relative importance of your ideas. The more important parts of your sentences should normally be the main clauses. Matters of secondary importance should usually be cast in the form of subordinate clauses, phrases, and sometimes even single words.

COORDINATION

When ideas are of roughly equal importance, coordination should be used. Coordination is the use of structurally equal sentence elements, such as two or more main clauses in a sentence, when ideas have about equal weight. (See PARALLELISM.) A common method of connecting main clauses and showing the logical relationship between them is the use of coordinating conjunctions (*and, but, or, nor, for, yet, so*):

* We appreciate the trust you have shown in us this past year, *and* we look forward to serving you even better in the year to come.

CORRECTING CHOPPINESS THROUGH SUBORDINATION

Excessive use of coordination results in choppy, stringy sentences (see CHOPPY SENTENCES) because the writer has failed to distinguish between ideas according to their importance:

* There was a computer breakdown today, *so* some of us lost several hours of important work, *and* all of us were inconvenienced in one minor way or another.

The use of coordination here (*so, and*) results in a choppy, stringy sentence that fails to stress any main idea. The skillful use of subordination puts these ideas into relative balance:

* *Because* there was a computer breakdown today, some of us lost several hours of important work, *while* all of us were inconvenienced in one minor way or another.

The main idea is now stated in a main clause ("some of us lost several hours of important work"), and the two lesser ideas are cast in subordinate clauses, one beginning with the subordinating conjunction *because*, the other with the subordinating conjunction *while*.

Subordinate clauses: Clauses (word groups containing both a subject and a verb) of this type most often begin with either a subordinating conjunction or a relative pronoun. *Because* is a common subordinating conjunction: I ate quickly *because* I feared arriving late. *That* is a common relative pronoun: I was afraid *that* I would arrive late. Here are lists of common *subordinators* that signal the beginning of a subordinate clause.

SUBORDINATING CONJUNCTIONS

after	if	until
although	in order that	when
as, as if	no matter how	whenever
as long as	once	where
as soon as	provided	wherever
as though	since	while
because	so that	why
before	though	
even though	unless	

that	who	whomever
what	whoever	whose
which	whom	

The following examples show means of improving choppy or stringy sentences through subordination:

POOR: There was a defect in the electronic circuit, *so* the digital display flickered.
BETTER: *Because* there was a defect in the electronic circuit, the digital display flickered.

POOR: Your copy of the project summary is enclosed. It is 18 pages in length. We are very pleased that you ordered it. [Short, choppy sentences.]
BETTER: We are very pleased to enclose a copy of the 18-page project summary that you ordered.

POOR: Your December 18 court date has been changed. I have to be in the state capital on business that day. January 16 at 9 a.m. is the new date. [Again, short, choppy sentences.]
BETTER: Since I have to be in the state capital on business on December 18, your court date has been changed to January 16 at 9 a.m.

T | TENSE

1. Use the proper order of tenses to express accurately the time relationships among your verbs.
2. Rely on your dictionary for the proper form of an irregular verb.
3. Avoid needless shifts in verb tenses.

The tense of a verb is the form that expresses a time-frame — past, present, or future — in which an event occurs. Within each time-frame there are variations in verb form that express more subtle time relations. For example, past tenses of the verb *to work* include *I worked* (simple past), *I have worked* (present perfect), and *I had worked* (past perfect). *Progressive* tenses include the participle *working*: *I have been working.* Present tense forms include *work, I am working.* Future tenses include *I shall (will) work, I shall (will) have worked,* and *I shall (will) be working.* And then there are the *conditional* tenses that express present, past, and future *possibilities* only: *I would work, I would have worked.* There are many more variations than these (*I shall have been working, I would have been working*), but these examples should serve for illustration.

1. SEQUENCE OF TENSES

All verbs in a sentence — and from one sentence to the next — should be in proper time relation to each other, or proper *sequence*.

If the actions in the main and subordinate clauses of a sentence occur at the same time, both verbs should be in the same tense.

* When the union members *voted,* they *approved* the pay increase unanimously.
* The new manager *acts* on a good suggestion as soon as you *make* it.

If the action in the main clause is *later* than the action of the subordinate clause, use the appropriate past tense in the subordinate clause.

* I *understand* that you *have* just *been awarded* a promotion. [The verb in the main clause, *understand,* is in the present tense. The verb in the subordinate clause, *have been awarded,* is in the present perfect and expresses a time just before the present tense of the main verb.]
* The jury *decided* that the defendant *had committed* the crime. [In this example the past perfect tense, *had committed,* in the subordinate clause, denotes a time before the simple past tense, *decided,* of the main clause.]

Habitual action, unchanging conditions, and permanent facts take the present tense, no matter what other tense is used in the sentence.

* Last week I *discovered* that he *knows* shorthand.
* I *have heard* that light *takes* about eight minutes to reach us from the sun.

Main verbs with infinitives. No matter what the tense of the main verb, use the *present* infinitive if its action is in the same time-frame as the main verb. Use the *past* infinitive if its action occurs before the main verb.

* I would like *to see* the new copier.
* I would have liked *to see* the new copier. [Although *to see* is the *present* infinitive, it is understood to be in the same time-frame, the past tense, of the main verb *would have liked.*]
* I would like *to have seen* the new copier. [The past infinitive, *to have seen,* refers to a time prior to the present tense, *would like,* of the main verb. Avoid doubling the past tense with the past infinitive: I would have liked to have seen the new play. Either *I would have liked to see* or *I would like to have seen* will do, but not both.]

2. IRREGULAR VERBS

Not all English verbs use the regular ending *–ed* to form the past tense (*turned*) and past participle (have *turned*). *Irregular* verbs are among the most common verbs used in the language. They form their past tenses and past participles in nonstandard ways that cannot be predicted from the present tense. *I drive,* for example, does not help you predict *I drove* or *I had driven.* If you are unsure of the correct verb form, look up the present-tense form of the verb in the dictionary. Listed right after it is the past tense and past participle.

Many problems with irregular verbs occur in combination with the use of contractions. (Avoid contractions in business writing unless they contribute to an informal or personal tone that you are striving for. See SINCERITY.) Note the following examples:

INCORRECT: If I'd *wrote* sooner, we would have received the order by now.
CORRECT: If I'd *written* sooner, we would have received the order by now. [The *I'd* is a contraction of *I had.* The helping verb *had* tells you that a past participle *written* — and not the past tense *wrote* — is needed.]

INCORRECT: I've *ran* that same memo off twice already.
CORRECT: I've *run* that same memo off twice already. [*I've,* the contraction of *I have,* indicates that the past participle *run* is needed here.]

3. TENSE SHIFTS

Although tense shifts may be logically needed to correspond with actual shifts in the time relations among your ideas, do not shift tenses needlessly. (See SHIFT IN POINT OF VIEW.)

ILLOGICAL SHIFT: She *sorts* the resistors according to their ohm rating and then *took* care to label each one.
REVISED: She sorts the resistors according to their ohm rating and then *takes* care to label each one.

CORRECT SHIFT: I *felt* exhausted yesterday, but today I *feel* peppy again. [An actual shift from past to present requires a shift in tenses.]

tact | TACT

Avoid statements likely to offend the reader.

When you speak, your voice, your facial expressions, your hand gestures, and your body language in general add emotional significance to your words well beyond the mere literal meaning of those words. As you can imagine, a spoken "I am sorry" can range in sound from truly contrite to viciously cutting. Unfortunately, the written word — without your bodily presence to accompany it — has to be taken at face value, and you must take special care that written statements that you mean kindly shall not be interpreted by your reader as cold or sarcastic. Always try to put yourself in your reader's place to check whether anything you write might lie open to misinterpretation. Even if you are provoked enough to *want* to offend the reader, avoid the temptation. Your organization can not afford to lose the goodwill of even one person.

Avoid expressions that accuse or criticize the reader. Many verbs with negative meanings preceded by a *you* or *your* have this effect: *you say, you claim, your complaint, you neglected, you forgot, you imply, you think, you failed to, you did not*. Try also to rephrase expressions that order the reader around: *you must, you have to*. (However, do not neglect the positive uses of *you*. See YOU-VIEWPOINT.) Equally tactless are bossy phrases with pretentious *we's: we must insist, we do not care to, we expect you to, we require, we demand*. (See also COURTESY.)

Here are some tactless statements together with tactful alternatives:

TACTLESS: Your order cannot be filled because you did not make clear just how many items you want and what their catalog numbers are.
TACTFUL: Enclosed is a catalog listing all our products and their catalog numbers. To ensure that we fill your order correctly, just use the enclosed order forms to indicate the catalog numbers and quantities of the items you want.

TACTLESS: How can we renew your insurance without the insurance policy number?
TACTFUL: We are very glad you decided to renew your insurance. Just send us the insurance policy number so that we can process your renewal quickly. You will find it printed on the top right hand corner of your policy.

Some writers requesting refunds or exchanges make the mistake of severely criticizing their readers. Such hostility actually decreases the writers' chance for prompt and fair reimbursement.

TACTLESS: You con artists have tried to sucker your last customer! The stereo I paid an outrageous $599 for at your crummy store does not work and probably never will. I demand my money back in full immediately, or I will drag you through every court in the country!
TACTFUL: Please refund the $599 I paid for a stereo at your store. I believe the stereo is defective. After following the installation directions step by step and after several hours of trying to figure out what is wrong, I have still been unable to get the stereo to operate as it should.

trans | TRANSITIONS

Connect your ideas smoothly and logically with proper transitions.

Transitions are logical bridges between ideas. A piece of writing that lacks transitions is bound to confuse the reader, even if the passage is only two sentences long:

* New York City is an interesting place to visit. Muggers and thieves roam the streets in some sections.

The writer seems to imply that a tourist would find New York interesting because of its muggers. Notice how the insertion of a transition sheds new light on the true connection between these sentences:

* New York City is an interesting place to visit *despite the fact that* muggers and thieves roam the streets in some sections.

Transitions are accomplished in four main ways:

1. through the use of certain standard transitional words or phrases
2. through repetition of key words or ideas
3. through pronouns
4. through demonstrative adjectives

1. TRANSITIONAL WORDS OR PHRASES

A special group of standard transitional words or phrases shows how a piece of writing progresses logically from one idea to the next. These expressions connect parts of sentences, connect one sentence to another, and also link paragraph to paragraph. They express logical relations between such ideas as addition (*also, besides, furthermore*); contrast (*but, however, on the contrary*); result (*therefore, consequently*); and space or time (*beyond, before, now, afterward*). The following lists include many of the most commonly used transitional expressions:

TRANSITIONAL WORDS

accordingly	further	nonetheless
actually	furthermore	notwithstanding
afterward	gradually	nor
again	hence	now
also	here	otherwise
and	however	second
before	indeed	similarly
beforehand	last	soon
besides	later	still
but	likewise	then
consequently	meanwhile	therefore
eventually	moreover	thereupon
finally	nevertheless	thus
first	next	too

TRANSITIONAL PHRASES

after all	for the time being	in spite of
all in all	for this purpose	in sum
all things considered	generally speaking	in the first place
and yet	in addition	in the meantime
as a result	in any case	in the past
at length	in any event	on the contrary
at the same time	in brief	on the other hand
by the same token	incidentally	on the whole
by the way	in contrast	to be sure
even so	in fact	to sum up
for example	in like manner	to this end
for instance	in other words	
for the most part	in short	

2. REPETITION OF KEY WORDS OR IDEAS

a. Repeat in the second sentence a key word used in the first.

- *Mary* worked here for seven years. It was not very long after *Mary* started that she was promoted to assistant manager.

b. Use a synonym of the key word.

- *Mary* worked here for seven years. As one of our most *efficient employees,* she was quickly promoted.

c. Use a word commonly paired with the key word, such as an antonym.

- It is *hot* in New Mexico. It is *cold* in Alaska.
- My *uncle* is a teacher. My *aunt* is a computer programmer.

d. Repeat key elements of phrasing or sentence structure (see PARALLELISM).

- *In the morning* I proofread the copy I wrote the day before. *In the afternoon* I write new copy.

e. Repeat key ideas.

- Now that I have discussed *the three accounting methods we can use,* I will point out the advantages we will gain by using *the last method.*

3. PRONOUNS

- *Mary* worked here for seven years. *She* was quickly promoted to assistant manager.
- We deeply regret our *mistake.* Please be sure *it* will not happen again.

4. DEMONSTRATIVE ADJECTIVES (THIS, THAT, THESE, THOSE)

• I have already written to you at length about the problems we are having with your new model. To prevent further misunderstandings, however, it appears that we should discuss *these* matters in person.

The failure to provide enough transitions severely damages the clarity, coherence, and smoothness of the following paragraph:

> Speeding up the assembly line has little effect on production. The workers get more tired more quickly. They require longer breaks more often. Frustration is a problem. Quality control is a problem. The chance of a missing part or an improperly sealed vacuum tube is greater. We should not do it.

Apart from a repeated key word and a pronoun or two, the paragraph is entirely lacking in transitional devices. Here is the same paragraph revised — and liberally provided with transitions so that the main idea and the supporting ideas can be clearly seen in relation to each other:

Repeat Key Idea — Speeding up the assembly line has little effect on production.

Trans. Word — *When the line goes faster,* the workers get more tired more quickly. Repeat Key Word

Pronoun — *Therefore, they* require longer breaks *more* often. *Those workers* Demons. Adj.

Repeat Key Idea — *who cannot quite keep up with the line* get frustrated quickly. Quality

Trans. Word — control is *also* a problem. *A faster line* increases the chance of a Repeat Key Idea

missing part or of an improperly sealed vacuum tube. *Thus,* we Trans. Word

should not *speed up the assembly line.* — Repeat Key Idea

---

trite | TRITENESS

Rewrite the marked passage to get rid of dull, overused expressions.

Trite means overused, uninteresting, ordinary, dull. Trite writing results from skimpy thinking or lazy phrasing. You can often weed out weak ideas if you think hard about your topic before you begin to write. In the same way, you can get rid of uninteresting, dead language if you deliberately employ the following few hints in choosing your words:

1. USE MORE LIVELY AND ACCURATE VERBS.

Avoid dead verbs such as *have, is,* or *are* when you can substitute something more colorful.

DEAD: We now *have* a new line of footwear.
BETTER: We *are introducing* a new line of footwear.

DEAD: Our main store *is* in the heart of Manhattan.
BETTER: *You will find* our main store in the heart of Manhattan.

In advertising and sales literature, use more flavorful, picturesque verbs.

TRITE: When you're *looking* for a thirst-quenching beer, think of Blecher's.
BETTER: When you're *panting* for a thirst-quenching beer, think of Blecher's.

TRITE: Nidas jogging shoes *fit firmly* without *being too tight.*
BETTER: Nidas jogging shoes *hug* but never *squeeze.*

2. USE CLEARER, MORE SPECIFIC, MORE COLORFUL NOUNS.

DEAD: You need several *things* before you tune up your car
BETTER: You need several *tools* before you tune up your car.

TRITE: You are welcome to enjoy our slimming *room* for one week free.
BETTER: You are welcome to enjoy our slimming *salon* for one week free.

3. USE MORE ACCURATE AND VIVID ADJECTIVES.

Wherever possible use fewer adjectives, but make each one count.

WEAK: She is a very *good, interesting,* and *imaginative* manager.
BETTER: She is a very *creative* manager.

Sometimes more adjectives are better — if they enable the reader to see more precisely what you have in mind.

TRITE: These chests all come in an *attractive* veneer.
BETTER: These chests all come in a *violet and mother-of-pearl* veneer.

It is often enough just to substitute one vivid adjective for a dull one.

DULL: A major advantage of our Greenlawn-model home is that every room in it is *large.*
BETTER: A major advantage of our Greenlawn-model home is that every room in it is *spacious.*

4. USE INTERESTING COMPARISONS.

Normally, business communication employs matter-of-fact, concrete, no-nonsense kinds of writing. Its purpose is practical — to get a message across as simply and as clearly as possible. There is little room in such writing for the highly imaginative language often found in literary works: puns, comparisons (including metaphors and similes), and other figures of speech. In advertising and sales literature, however, the practical purpose of selling something is accomplished to a greater or lesser extent by creating a persuasive emotional climate — and that is managed through the skillful use of colorful and creative forms of expression.

The use of fresh and vivid comparisons is often essential to the effectiveness of sales literature. A good comparison often works better than a whole sentence of description or explanation. Comparisons using *like* or *as* are called similes: A pillow *as* soft *as* a satin-covered cloud. Comparisons without *like* or *as* are called metaphors: We offer you the *Rolls-Royce* of computers at *Volkswagen* prices.

Avoid clichés. If you must use comparisons, stay away from clichés. Clichés are comparisons and other figures of speech that have become so popular and overused that they have long lost their original freshness and fail to excite a positive response in the reader. There are numerous clichés. Here is a sampling (in italics):

- *The tide is turning* in favor of our products.
- Our reputation for good service is *as old as the hills*.
- Our fully stocked shelves are *as neat as a pin*.
- Gropp will *move mountains* to insure your comfort.
- Why buy *a pig in the poke* if you can buy Kardel's?
- A Life-Shield policy will make you, too, *as snug as a bug in a rug*.

CLICHE: At long last, *the tide is beginning to turn* in our favor.
FRESHER: At long last, the rain is beginning to patter on our parched front lawn.

CLICHE: Our luggage is *as light as a feather*.
FRESHER: A two-year-old can lift our luggage with a pinky.

5. AVOID THE HACKNEYED EXPRESSIONS OF BUSINESS CORRESPONDENCE.

Read the following glossary of trite expressions, take note of the suggested alternatives, and try to avoid these commonplaces in your next letter or report:

TRITE EXPRESSION	SUGGESTED ALTERNATIVE
1. acknowledge receipt of	1. we received
2. allow me to say that	2. (omit entirely)
3. as the case may be	3. (omit entirely)
4. at present	4. now
5. attached please find	5. I have included
6. at your convenience	6. when you have time
7. avail yourself of this opportunity	7. take this opportunity
8. beg to differ	8. I disagree
9. be that as it may	9. (omit entirely)

TRITE EXPRESSION	SUGGESTED ALTERNATIVE
10. contents noted	10. I have noted
11. deem it advisable	11. believe you should
12. enclosed please find	12. I have enclosed
13. henceforth	13. from now on
14. heretofore	14. until now
15. herewith	15. (omit entirely)
16. hitherto	16. until now
17. I have your letter of (date)	17. (omit entirely)
18. in accordance with your request	18. as you requested
19. in due time (or in due course)	19. (give the date)
20. in the amount of	20. for
21. in re	21. concerning
22. in reply to your letter	22. (omit entirely)
23. it has come to my attention	23. I have learned, I have noticed
24. kindly	24. please
25. our records indicate	25. according to our records (or omit entirely)
26. per capita	26. for each person
27. per diem	27. by the day
28. per your request	28. as you requested
29. permit me to say	29. (omit entirely)
30. please be advised	30. (omit entirely)
31. please don't hesitate to call upon us should you have any questions	31. just call if you have a question
32. pursuant to your inquiry	32. in answer to your question
33. take pleasure	33. we are glad
34. take the liberty of saying	34. (omit entirely)
35. thanking you in advance	35. thank you
36. under separate cover	36. in another envelope
37. we are in receipt of	37. we received
38. we regret to inform you	38. we are sorry
39. you claim	39. thank you for telling us
40. your complaint	40. thank you for telling us

The following example shows how the omission of trite expressions can improve a business letter:

TRITE: We are in receipt of your letter dated May 8. Pursuant to your inquiry, we regret to inform you that Catalog No. 119GH is out of stock at the present time. Our records indicate that we can expect a new supply in due course, and we will ship your order as soon as possible.

IMPROVED: Thank you for sending us your May 8 order for one Catalog No. 119GH. This item is out of stock right now, but we expect a new supply in two weeks. As soon as the bedspreads arrive, we will ship your order.

Stick to the point within each of your paragraphs.

A unified paragraph develops only one main idea. Every sentence contributes to the main idea. If your paragraph lacks unity, look back at your main point again. Does each sentence contribute meaningfully toward fleshing out that point? If any sentence drifts away from your main objective, drop it or change it. (See also IRRELEVANT and PARAGRAPH.)

SAMPLE PARAGRAPH LACKING UNITY:

> There are important advantages in using staff planners to recommend business action and originate strategy. By hiring individuals solely to forecast, form policy, and aid in decision making, managers are assured of careful planning. These individuals are not encumbered by other duties, nor are they biased by membership in any one department or by attachment to any function other than planning. Bias can wreak havoc in planning objectives. Many poor decisions have been made as a result of not seeing the whole picture but of planning merely to safeguard or foster one aspect of an organization. For instance, the Marc-Lessner Corporation recently decided against computerizing its poorly organized inventory because the manager of the Inventory Control Department wanted to protect his job and those of his staff. The long-term effects of this decision will surely be increased customer dissatisfaction with order-filling promptness.

ANALYSIS: This paragraph gets away from its writer. It begins with a discussion of staff planners but ends with an illustration of biased decision making. The writer who wanders from the subject does not have a firm grip on the topic. To keep to the point, you should write a clear topic sentence for every paragraph, then check each paragraph to be sure it actually develops what you say it will develop. To improve the sample paragraph, all you need to do is remove the irrelevant sentences.

SAMPLE PARAGRAPH REVISED:

> There are important advantages in using staff planners to recommend business action and originate strategy. By hiring individuals solely to forecast, form policy, and aid in decision making, managers are assured of careful planning. These individuals are not encumbered by other duties, nor are they biased by membership in any one department or by attachment to any function other than planning. Thus, staff planners are able to see the whole picture. They can plan for the good of the entire organization, not just one part.

Avoid vagueness and undefined abstract expressions in your writing. Strive for concreteness.

Imagine the following statement made to a company official in charge of disbursing funds:

* We need to hire an outside consultant who will help us improve our office procedures.

If this is the whole message, the official who receives it will probably regard it as too *vague* to act on. If, however, an office manager writes to a superior in the following more concrete way, positive results are likely to occur sooner:

* Our entire system of office routines has been thrown into confusion by the recent introduction of word-processing stations, and we need the advice of an outside consultant to help our willing office staff take advantage of the new technology and thereby improve our productivity.

The vagueness of the first message is now replaced by the concreteness of the second. You gain concreteness by using specific facts and figures, details that create a clear image, and vivid, direct language.

The problem of vagueness may involve not only whole communications but even the choice of individual words. Certain common adjectives are often too vague to be useful to someone who needs more precise information: *good, large, many, most, nice, short, high, small, tall, slow.* What is tall for a five-foot person may be short for a six-footer.

VAGUE: I can assure you that our copier gives good results.
CONCRETE: The new Loflin copier produces letter-quality photostats at a rate of 30 per minute and can collate a 50-page document in less than 10 seconds. [We now know what the vague *good* means.]

VAGUE: These savings certificates earn you high interest.
CONCRETE: These savings certificates earn you high interest: 10.6 percent compounded every three months for two years.

ABSTRACT EXPRESSIONS

A special variety of vagueness results from the misuse of abstract expressions such as *beauty, morality, democracy, progress, corruption, individualism, efficiency, Americanism.* Expressions such as these mean different things to different people. Unfortunately, they sometimes have very little specific meaning to the writer who uses them — and they may be used out of laziness or prejudice as a substitute for dealing with the real issues these terms *appear* to describe.

UNDEFINED ABSTRACTIONS: Our new model K43 opaque projector does cost somewhat more than the obsolete K42, but we believe that the price difference is modest when you consider the vast *progress* we have made in increasing product *efficiency.*

CONCRETE: Our new model K43 opaque projector does cost somewhat more than the obsolete K42, but we believe that the modest price difference of 8 percent is more than made up for by an advanced design that guarantees bright, razor-sharp images from center to edge at a projection distance of 12 feet, an increase of 33 percent in projection efficiency over the K42.

---

var | VARIETY IN SENTENCE PATTERNS

Achieve a smoother style through varying your sentence patterns.

If you vary the length and pattern of your sentences, your writing will sound more rhythmic and interesting, less choppy and monotonous. You can make endless pleasing combinations out of four basic sentence patterns: simple, compound, complex, and compound-complex.

1. SIMPLE SENTENCE

A simple sentence consists of only one main clause.

* Henry Ford pioneered the mass production of automobiles.

The basis of a simple sentence, or main clause, is a subject — *Henry Ford* — a verb — *pioneered* — and, often but not always, a direct object — *the mass production of automobiles.*

2. COMPOUND SENTENCE

A compound sentence is made up of two or more main clauses usually joined by a coordinating conjunction (*and, but, or, nor, for, yet*).

* The last applicant was by far the most qualified, but the second one seemed to have a more suitable personality for the job. [Notice the comma before the coordinating conjunction *but.* See COMMA, Rule 2.]

3. COMPLEX SENTENCE

A complex sentence contains one main clause and one or more subordinate clauses. A subordinate clause (see SUBORDINATION) contains a subject and a verb, but it cannot stand alone as a sentence because it begins with a subordinating conjunction (*after, before, because, if, when*) or a relative pronoun (*that, which, who, whom, whose, whoever, whomever*):

- Because we misplaced the bill of lading, we cannot trace the shipment.

        Subordinate Clause   Main Clause

- We cannot trace the shipment whose bill of lading was misplaced.

       Main Clause   Subordinate Clause

4. COMPOUND-COMPLEX SENTENCE

A compound-complex sentence is, as its name implies, a combination of a compound and a complex sentence. It contains at least two main clauses (compound) and at least one subordinate clause (complex):

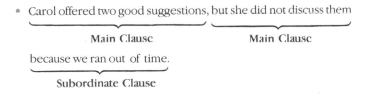

- Carol offered two good suggestions, but she did not discuss them

       Main Clause   Main Clause

  because we ran out of time.

      Subordinate Clause

NOTE: If you combine a series of simple sentences into a pattern that includes a variety of sentence types, your writing will become more interesting, less monotonous or choppy.

SERIES OF SIMPLE SENTENCES: We have special instructions for overseas shipments. First, we wrap each wattmeter in thick plastic. Then we place it in a cardboard box. Next, we add styrofoam. We completely cover the meter with it. Then this box is packed in a wooden crate. Last, we stencil the outside with the contents and address.

REVISED USING VARIETY OF SENTENCE TYPES: We have special instructions for overseas shipments [*simple*]. First, we wrap each wattmeter in thick plastic, and then we place it in a cardboard box [*compound*]. Next, we add styrofoam until the meter is completely covered [*complex*]. Then this box is packed in a wooden crate with the contents and address stenciled on the outside [*simple*].

The first paragraph consists of seven simple sentences that create a monotonous, choppy rhythm. The revised version combines the ideas into four sentences, including simple, compound, and complex types; and the result is more rhythmic and readable than the first.

Use well-known words that you might encounter in an actual conversation. Avoid jargon. Write on a level your reader can comfortably handle.

Too many business writers forget that their purpose is to communicate and build goodwill. Instead, they write letters or reports whose pretentious, jargon-filled diction is meant to impress. Most readers, however, will feel slighted or intimidated by such vocabulary, and they will resent the writer accordingly. (See also TACT and CONVERSATIONAL.)

Always choose a level of vocabulary that your readers will be comfortable with. For general readers, this prescription means simple conversational language and sentences with an average length of twelve to eighteen words. Of course, shorter and longer sentences are desirable for variety. (See VARIETY IN SENTENCE PATTERNS.) Raise your vocabulary above the general level only if you are sure your audience will find it easy to understand. Never, however, indulge in bureaucratic gobbledygook, as in the following example:

PRETENTIOUS: Notwithstanding variable factors for which no precise determination can be assigned, proprietary implementation of the proposed marketing strategy will commence this January.
APPROPRIATE VOCABULARY: Whatever else happens, we will launch our advertising campaign this January.

CONDESCENDINGLY LOW: There is a little metal stick on the side of the typewriter. Put it on the number 1 if you want to type with no lines left between your typed lines. Put the stick on 2 if you want to leave one blank line between your typed lines.
APPROPRIATE VOCABULARY: Move the spacing lever on the side of the typewriter to 1 for single space or 2 for double space.

AVOIDING JARGON

A common vocabulary problem is the overuse of jargon, the technical terminology of a particular field of specialization. Nearly every occupation has its jargon words: *escrow, accrual,* and *bond indenture* in banking; *annuitant, actuary tables,* and *beneficiary* in insurance; and *rationalization, compartmentalization,* and *projection* in psychology. Never use jargon in a general audience communication unless you define it for your readers. After all, many jargon words are not even listed in most dictionaries. Even when writing to specialists in a given field, use a word less specialized than the jargon term if your message would thereby come across in a manner at least equally precise, clear, and effective.

JARGON: The end-user can configure the proprietary accounting cycle within the parameters of this flexible software.

APPROPRIATE VOCABULARY: This program allows you to set up your company's individual accounting system on a computer.

wdy | WORDINESS

Eliminate unnecessary, repetitious, and irrelevant wording. Be concise.

Just as you do, your readers often feel pressed for time and appreciate brevity in the communications they receive. If they can avoid doing so, many readers will not even bother to read through a very long letter or memo and will give up after staggering through a windy paragraph or so. Effective business communication is concise. Make every word count, but do not go to the other extreme and write telegrams: clarity, grace, and courtesy are as important as bare-bone meaning.

There are four major categories of wordiness:

1. unnecessary information, such as an excess of data or examples, overlong introductions, or irrelevant material (See IRRELEVANT.)
2. unnecessary jargon (See VOCABULARY.)
3. repetition (See REPETITION)
4. unnecessary words

The first three types of wordiness are discussed elsewhere in this book. This section confines itself to the fourth.

UNNECESSARY WORDS

Avoid certain common expressions that simply take up space out of proportion to their meaning. Substitute briefer expressions:

WORDY	CONCISE
along the line of	about
due to the fact that (he resigned)	because (he resigned)
for a long period of time	for a long time
for the price of ($150)	for ($150)
for the purpose of	for
in spite of the fact that (he left)	despite (his leaving)
in the amount of ($5)	for ($5)
in the event that	if

NOTE: See also the long list of expressions, many of them wordy, under TRITENESS.

Many writers tend to use too many words in the first draft. Edit your own writing by crossing out excess verbiage, simplifying unnecessarily complicated constructions, and rewriting for conciseness.

WORDY: This letter is to inform you that your two brand-new Officemate chairs will be carefully packed and then promptly shipped to you on or before the date of June 18.
REVISED: Your two Officemate chairs will be shipped by June 18.

WORDY: Your request for an appointment with Mrs. Golladay has been received, and she tells me that she will be most happy to see you this Tuesday at about 10 o'clock in the morning if this is a convenient time for you.
REVISED: If convenient, Mrs. Golladay will be happy to see you this Tuesday morning at 10.

WORDY: This durable steel check-storage box will keep your checks safe from fire and heat damage and will hold up to 10,000 checks at a time.
REVISED: This fireproof steel check-storage box holds up to 10,000 checks.

you | YOU-VIEWPOINT

Write from the reader's point of view
rather than your own or your company's.

Make your business writing more effective by using the words *you* or *your* wherever possible instead of *we* or *our.* Show your readers that you are thinking of them instead of yourself (see also READER ADVANTAGE).

COMPANY VIEWPOINT: Under our warranty we do cover the cost of your car repair.
YOU-VIEWPOINT: Your warranty does cover the cost of your car repair.

COMPANY VIEWPOINT: We now offer our easy-cleaning cookware in kitchen-coordinated colors.
YOU-VIEWPOINT: Complement your kitchen decor with our easy-cleaning cookware.

COMPANY VIEWPOINT: We must have a deposit before we can process your order.
YOU-VIEWPOINT: Your deposit will esure speedy processing of your order.

CAUTION: Do *not* use a you-viewpoint when your reader has made a mistake (see TACT).

TACTLESS: You have allowed your coupon to expire.
TACTFUL: Regrettably, this coupon has expired.

PROGRESS CHART

You will find the columns below useful for recording the errors you have made in your written assignments throughout the term. Use the first column to list the errors in your first assignment, the second column for the errors in your second assignment, etc. For convenience, use the correction symbols only, and next to each, write how many times that particular error occurs in that assignment: for example, FRAG (2). You should be able to see your progress — and your main problems — revealed more and more as the term goes on.

Business English _____

ASGT. # DATE GRADE	ASGT. # DATE GRADE	ASGT. # DATE GRADE	ASGT. # DATE GRADE	ASGT. # DATE GRADE	ASGT. # DATE GRADE

ASGT. # DATE GRADE	ASGT. # DATE GRADE	ASGT. # DATE GRADE	ASGT. # DATE GRADE	ASGT. # DATE GRADE	ASGT. # DATE GRADE

SPELLING PROGRESS CHART

List in the columns below the correct forms for the words you misspell on each assignment. Your chart will develop into an excellent diagnosis of your spelling problems.

Business English _____

ASGT. # DATE GRADE	ASGT. # DATE GRADE	ASGT. # DATE GRADE	ASGT. # DATE GRADE	ASGT. # DATE GRADE	ASGT. # DATE GRADE

ASGT. # DATE GRADE	ASGT. # DATE GRADE	ASGT. # DATE GRADE	ASGT. # DATE GRADE	ASGT. # DATE GRADE	ASGT. # DATE GRADE